Scream if you want to Run *FASTER!!*

By Julie Creffield

Scream if you want to Run *Faster!!*

Copyright: Julie Creffield
Published: 9th January 2017
Publisher: The Fat Girls' Guide to Running

Find out more about the author and upcoming books at www.toofattorun.co.uk or on twitter @fattymustrun

For my daughter, Rose.

She drives me to push hard and make stuff happen,
but also teaches me to slow down a bit occasionally
so that I don't miss out on all the good stuff.

Table of Contents

Extra Race Day Tactics

The final word

Welcome to my World

*"If you don't like the road you're walking,
start paving another one." – **Dolly Parton***

I stood there in total disbelief. "OMG, ain't they cold?" I asked myself as I nervously shifted my weight from side to side and blew hot air into my cupped hands in an attempt to keep warm.

Why had I not thought to bring gloves? I shifted my hands from in front of me to cover my freezing boobs, which were now starting to make a bit of a show of themselves.

"God it's flipping freezing" I muttered under my breath, shaking my head that I was actually here and not still in bed.

Most normal people have a lie in on a Sunday, but not me 'cos obviously I'm not normal.

It was mid November in 2010 and I was at the start of a local 10K race in Victoria Park, East London, led by a local running club with the name 'Harriers' in the title. That should have been enough of a clue, but back then I was completely clueless on all that kind of stuff.

I loved running, but I still didn't know how it all worked. Sound familiar?

I'd arrived a full twenty minutes ago, full of confidence to collect my race number from the small building, which served as race HQ. But now, as I stood there in my slightly too tight t-shirt and equally snug-around-the-waist running leggings, I was in a bit of a panic. I surveyed the crowd looking for anyone who looked remotely like me. "Where's the fat person, where's the fat person, where's the fat person?" I said in my head, scanning the bodies before me and accepting that I was the only even slightly overweight person here.

"Ok, are there any kids, old people, disabled people, come on?" I was starting to dread what was about to come next.

Because just ahead of me were about 300 identically slim and white middle-aged men in short shorts (no I mean REALLY short shorts) warming up by running up and down the same bit of path, plus a few really athletic looking women attaching their race numbers with care and stretching. Oh and then there was me in my size 18 body, a newcomer to the sport, sticking out like a sore thumb in the brand new running shoes I'd treated myself to yesterday from Sports Direct.

Clearly I didn't get the memo that suggested this was a serious race. A race for proper, hardcore athletes. A race that, little did I know, was about to change my life FOREVER!

This wasn't my first running event though, oh no. Although I described myself earlier as a beginner, I had in fact been running on and off for a couple of years. I had even done a few park runs and a number of other races, but this was something else completely.

I'd never seen such a serious looking bunch of athletes before in my life. Well, aside from when I watched the athletics on the telly.

The atmosphere was strange.

Nobody spoke to me.

In fact, nobody even looked at me.

I was positioned right at the back, but even still.

Before I knew it we were about to get going and everyone shuffled forward and started fiddling with their watches. The grumpy looking starter official for the race kicked things off with one of those pressurized horn thingies, which startled me somewhat, but I took the cue as presented and started to move. But literally within the first 30 seconds I was left for dust, despite going off faster than I normally would.

All I could do was watch as the small crowd ahead of me disappeared into the distance as I plodded on, trying not to be too disheartened.

The race was 3 loops of just one side of Victoria Park. Perhaps I'd catch someone up as they lost their puff later in the race, I thought. You know, like the tortoise and the hare and all of that, but after a while I couldn't even see any runners ahead of me to chase.

The park was still in full use by other park users and every now and again there was a strategically placed volunteer steward, identifiable only by their luminous tabards. They were not like the foam-hand-wearing, whooping, smiling and cheering volunteers I had experienced in other races. These guys looked like they would rather have been anywhere else than here on this cold, blustery Sunday morning.
A bit like I was feeling actually.

I'm not going to lie, I felt a little embarrassed by the fact that I was quite obviously a lot slower than the other runners in the field. I'm not sure I realised by how much though at this point. That shame was to come much later.

So I did the first lap in around twenty-five minutes. This was pretty good going for me, I thought. The second lap was a little trickier, as the faster runners started passing me at speed. A few even shouting for me to get out of their way.

Oops, which side of the path should I be running on again?

"Keep going Julie," I kept telling myself as I made my way around the familiar park. "Just keep going, this is your race. You have paid the entry like everyone else. And someone has to come last, right?"

Glancing at my watch (not a sports watch by the way, just a normal every day watch my Mum had bought for me last Christmas), I figured I was actually running OK speed-wise, roughly 4 miles in around 45 minutes. A little quicker than normal even.
But by the time I passed the finishing area for the second time it looked like most of the runners had finished. In fact, the stewards looked baffled as I passed them for the 3rd time, wondering where I was off to.

But I was determined to do my 3 laps no matter what and no matter how long it took me. I mean, it's not like there was a cut-off time advertised and I didn't have anyone waiting for me to finish.

So I just kept plodding on, doing the best I could. Smiling at and thanking the volunteers as I went, with little positive effect it seemed. I didn't walk though, even though at times I wanted to. I couldn't be seen to be walking. No, that would be just too much, the final stage on my embarrassment scale.

One foot in front of the other, keep plodding, breathing deep and long, using my arms to power me round as much as I could. Ignore the pain in your hip, the tightening in your calves, not much further.

The stewards looked pretty relieved to see me come past for the 3rd time, as one by one they gathered their belongings and made their way back to their colleagues. I felt a little guilty that they had to wait for me. But hey, this is what they sign up to, right?

Hmm, I wasn't so sure. Especially as the last few stewards had actually already left their positions by the time I got there, which perhaps should have been the first clue as to what I could expect a little further ahead.

My face was bright red. I could feel my cheeks burning.

My hair was dripping with sweat, my mascara was probably half way down my face
too. Which is never a good look.

My cotton t-shirt was soaked through and had ridden up in a somewhat revealing way in this, the final dash.

Oh, and I could just about feel the beginnings of some unfortunate chafing in my nether regions too.

But I was almost done.

Well almost.

I would be finishing soon. There would be water and maybe even something to eat and then I could admire my medal. Take a couple of red-faced selfies and go home feeling proud of myself.

However, this was not to be.

Because sadly I arrived at the finish line to find the finish line was no longer there and neither was anyone else. No volunteers, no race officials, no medals, not even any runners lurking around stretching.

It was like I was a ghost runner, like I didn't exist. Like I wasn't even a participant somehow. Surely someone must have known I was still out there?

I felt a little numb.

No water.

Nobody to say well done.

Not even a bloody banana.

What a numpty.

If my face was red before, it was a strange shade of beetroot now. And it was starting to actually throb, along with the growing lump in my throat and great, my eyes had started to well up too.

Don't cry Julie. Do NOT cry!

After catching my breath and rearranging my kit I looked at my watch and it told me it was eighteen minutes past 10. The race had started bang on 9 o'clock so it had taken me roughly an hour and eighteen minutes to get round. Which I think at that point in my running career was close to my PB for 10K.

Was I really that slow?

Did the organisers simply give up waiting for me in the cold? Had they forgotten I
was still out there on the course? Or were they just like, "Fuck it, we're off. She's just too slow."

Who knows.

I sheepishly made my way back to the Clubhouse where I had left my warm clothes.
Ah, so this was where all the runners were congregating. Keeping themselves warm with cups of tea and comparisons of times. If I could have avoided this bit I would have done, trust me, and I avoided making eye contact with anyone. I fiddled with my safety pins and race number to remove all evidence that I was actually a participant.

Too embarrassed to hang around, I unlocked my bike and cycled home as quickly as I could manage with my rather fatigued legs.

Phew.

What a race!

On the way home I kept jumping between embarrassment, anger and then a bit of laughter. It could only happen to me. I mean, surely this kind of thing doesn't happen to other women? Surely I am not the only fat, slow runner out there?

Sitting on the sofa in my flat with a cup of tea to warm me up while the bath ran, I did a quick Google search on my phone for the term "FAT Runner", which brought up some interesting articles about running for weight loss, but nothing much about the realities of being an overweight runner.

Seriously, it's hard to believe now with the wealth of books and blogs and campaigns out there about plus-size fitness, or even just fitness for people who don't look like supermodels. It shows how far the movement has come in the last few years.

Because that afternoon, after a longer than normal bath and a low calorie tasteless microwave meal, 'The Fat Girls' Guide to Running' blog was born. And life took a whole new direction for me.

So let's get this straight. I had never blogged before, ever. I literally just followed the instructions on a "How to start a blog" article I happened to find online. It was all a bit impulsive, all a bit random. But it was anonymous back then, no photo of me and no reference of my name so kind of no risk. If it was shit I could just pull it down after a few weeks. For the purposes of this new blogging project I was just a fat female runner, I could have been any fat female runner. And that was kind of the point.

Who would have thought it, hey? That my little ol' blog would become what it is today - a movement that has inspired thousands of women across the globe to take up or stick with running.

I truly believe that random day 6 years ago happened for a reason, because when I came dead last in a race for the first time EVER something shifted in me. A light went on, a fire started to burn in my belly. And no, it wasn't indigestion.

I simply felt compelled to write about my experiences of being a plus-size, slower- than-average runner and the rest, as they say, is history.

672 blog posts' worth of history.

4 million hits on a website worth of history.

Over a million unique visitors and thousands of customers and clients.

And a whole heap of experiences, opportunities and new friendships created in the process. And all off the back of that horrid, embarrassing race.

See, there really is no such thing as failure ladies, just opportunities to learn and grow as a person. And of course you have all those embarrassing and slightly humorous experiences to add to your life story, a story that might inspire someone else to make a change in their life too.

Who knows?

So what's the deal with this book?

The secret of getting ahead is getting started. — *Sally Berger*

Welcome to Scream If You Want to Run Faster.

This is the book that is absolutely going to change how you run forever by getting you as close as possible to that fantastic 5K PB you have always dreamed of.

That sure is a big claim, right? But what did you expect?

Big girl, big claims, what can I say?!

Look, I know it is a little funny relying on a book about improving your speed by a runner who herself takes close to 6 hours to complete a marathon. A runner that is the first to admit that she is also a plodder, a slogger and some times even a walker.

A runner that is seen by some in the running world as a bit of a joke, or a bit of a gimmick.

But bear with me here, for what I lack in actual speed I more than make up for in my absolute understanding of the desire we all share as plus-sized runners to be able to run faster. Plus, these are tried and tested techniques with a whole heap of evidence to back up my claims.

This book was of course written with larger ladies in mind, but actually it's not just us more robust ladies that are concerned with speed. Most recreational runners feel a pressure to run at a certain pace in order to feel like a 'proper' runner. It's a universal problem.

A problem that is compounded by the cultures and structures that the traditional running world has created for us over the last few centuries. But a problem I hope to tackle with this book. Because as Confucius said all those years ago:

It doesn't matter how slow you go,
so long as you do not stop.

When I asked my Facebook community what the downside of being a slower runner was, I was simply bombarded with hundreds of messages outlining how frustrating and unfair it can be;

- **Not being able to run with friends**
- **Being too slow to join a running club**
- **Coming last at races**
- **Events being packed up before you finish**
- **Water, medals and goodie bags running out**
- **Keeping volunteers (and family members) waiting**
- **Having to cope with hecklers**
- **Being overtaken by people twice your age or twice as young**

The list was endless. In one post on Facebook I had over 200 comments, with some rather funny and lighthearted stories, but also some shocking ones which makes you wonder how and why slow runners would ever go out and run again.

"Having the finish line arch taken down just as you round the corner at the end of a half marathon. The race director said to me his team had been out since 5am, but it's not like I hadn't been too, collecting my race packet and then running the 13.1 miles. Needless to say I will never do that race again"

"I've had road sweepers shouting at me to get out their way so they can clear up, and sweeper staff asking constantly if I am ready to give up yet. Why would I give up? I'm slow, but I trained for this."

"People who shout "you can do it, you can do it", so bloody patronizing. NEWSFLASH: this IS me doing it."

The stories were so familiar to me, as trust me I have been there and it's why I simply had to write this book.

Yes, there are a hundred and one running books out there for beginners. Lots of autobiographical memoir-type books showcasing the inspirational stories of triumph over adversity, but what about a book that actually helps women make real progress with their running?

A book that helps you to run faster, but without the scientific bullshit designed to baffle you and make it sound harder than it actually is.

It's not that I am dismissing the science behind athletics, I am just saying that most of us don't care about the technical terms for things, and are often scared off by all the jargon. We just want practical advice that we can put into action.

I knew this book needed to be different from what was already out there on the market, which for everyday runners on the subject of speed was actually quite thin on the ground. It had to look different and it had to read differently. Ultimately it had to make women behave differently. For me to achieve the massive goal which I had set out for the book, I am counting on you guys to give it your all.

"Scream if you want to run faster will help a million women feel more confident about their running simply by helping them to run a little faster"

These were the early notes I scribbled in red pen in my notebook more than 3 years ago when I first got the idea for the book, a book that would give women;

- **Hope**
- **A sense that they are not alone**
- **Coping strategies**
- **Tools to seek real improvement**

And most importantly

- **An opportunity to share their progress with other likeminded women.**

But what's with the name? 'Scream if you want to run faster'? Couldn't I have called it something normal, like 'How to Get Faster for Fat Women'? Or 'How to Improve Your Running Speed in 60 days if You Are Heavy Set'?

I'm only mucking about of course, but I knew it needed to stand out. Do you know how many running books there are on Amazon these days? Everyone and their dog (like seriously) are publishing them!

I am a creative kind of girl.

I don't always follow the rules or do things the way everyone else does and I knew I wanted a title which would stand out and really talk to my ladies. In fact, I wanted it to scream and shout from the shelf at them;

"Coeeey, over here ladies. I CAN HELP YOU GET FASTER. Honestly!"

And that's when the title came to me.

SCREAM if you want to RUN FASTER – 'cos we all do really, don't we? Even if we don't want to admit it.

The thing with the action of screaming is you can't do it half-heartedly can you?

I mean, just try it. Next time you are in the bedroom in the throes of passion, try screaming quietly. OK perhaps that's not the most appropriate example. What about when you stub your toe on the bed in the morning? Well the scream is just instantaneous, right? You can't stifle. And let's not talk about childbirth!

John Lennon summed this up perfectly; *"When you're drowning, you don't say 'I would be incredibly pleased if someone would have the foresight to notice me drowning and come and help me,' you just scream."*

So scream if you must. Because it is that kind of passion I need to see from you, maybe even aggression. Find that power inside of you and that drive that is going to stop you plodding and get you pounding.

Sound like hard work?

GOOD!

I wanted a title that left you under no illusion that the process would be tough. It would require you to dig deep, face your fears and discover the kickarse side of your personality. Which, who knows, might even be useful in other areas of your life too.

You just have to suck it up and get the job done, just how Wonder Woman would or She-Ra. No procrastination, no pussy footing around, just put on your big girl pants, your best "I don't care stare" and get out there and get the job done.

A few years back when my business was just starting out, I wanted to test the idea of an online running club. I had no marketing budget, no money to design a snazzy membership site, but what I did have was a couple of hundred followers on social media and the enthusiasm to try something new.

So I came up with 'BISH, BASH, BOSH', a monthly challenge delivered on Facebook. The premise was simple; each day for 30 days I would post a simple fitness, food or fun task and after the ladies completed it they would post 'Bish, Bash, Bosh' on social media to signal its completion.

No discussion, no excuses, just a simple way of saying I want to be accountable and I want to make progress. It felt very dynamic, a bit gung ho and Superhero-like. This tribe of women out in the world doing squats in the loos, and walking home from the office in their skirt suits and trainers. Workout warriors!

We now have hundreds of women in our online running club, The Clubhouse, and the 'Bish, Bash, Bosh' attitude lives on in our closed Facebook Group. Women use the tool of social media to encourage and motivate each other with virtual boots-up-the-backside and sparkling emoji celebrations upon their return.

I know just how important making improvements in speed can be for a beginner. It can often be the difference between tentatively dipping your toe in the sport and sticking with it for the long term. The frustration of never seeing any improvement in running times can be so demoralising. It can also make you feel quite ostracised by the wider running community.

I can absolutely help you run faster with my techniques, but I'm sorry to have to break it to you; you will have to do some of the work too. You have to approach each technique with the same amount of vigor as the previous one, attacking it as if your life depended on it. And it might one day (but more of that later).

Some caveats first though. This book is not for you if you:

- Are an elitist running snob (yep you know who you are!)
- Can already run a 5K in under 25 minutes

- Are in any way interested in biomechanics or the science of running
- A bloke. OK I know I shouldn't discriminate, but I am writing this for women really. I don't have much experience of being an over weight, slow, MALE runner and everyone always says write what you know.

But if you are a female runner, new or returning to the sport, or a frustrated old timer annoyed with your seeming inability to get faster, despite putting in the time and effort, I can and will help you.

Firstly, I can help you unlock the mental block you may have on running at pace and then I will help you face the denial you may be in as to why you fail to see improvement, despite your efforts. This bit might be painful, but I will try to be kind.

Then I will give you the practical tools you need to break down your current training programme, with tips and tricks to freshen things up so you can move forward in a more proactive and positive way.

The book includes case studies and anecdotes from real women from my online community who took part in a pilot with me to test the principles. They will talk about what improving their speed meant to them and what it took to actually implement the techniques.

Disclaimer - This book is not a magic wand that will transform your race times without any hard work on your behalf. You have to do the work.

Should I read the book in a specific way?

YES. Read it cover to cover, and please try this without eye rolling, or attitudes of "well that's silly" or "Well, I'm not gonna be able to do that". I told you this book is different, so you can expect some mindset trickery and calls to action to speak to your inner self. You know, the one you tend to silence most of the time?

Please try and read with an open mind and a 'can do' attitude. Make notes if you want. Scribble on the pages. Stick post-it notes around your home. Whatever it takes for the theory to sink in.

You might be compelled to try out a few of the techniques in isolation before going for it fully with the more structured 60 day programme, and that is fine. But remember, the specifics of the programme help you see the most amount of progress in one fell swoop; fiddling around the edges might give you some small gains, but nothing like committing fully.

Take special note of my 3 Secret Weapons, found towards the end of the book. If you implement nothing else, these will get you moving in a new gear no doubt.

So yes, read it through. All of it.

Digest the theory for a bit and then spend an afternoon hatching your plan. Make a start when you feel like you have the commitment, resolve and energy to give it your all. But please don't read the book and do nothing.

I will give you more details of the 60-day plan later, plus I will explain my 3 Secret Weapons when it comes to increasing speed and also you will find a link to some FREE downloadable resources I have created to help you plan and implement your successful journey to FASTER.

You have to keep the faith though. Mindset is everything. As Walt Disney said; *"If you can believe it you can achieve it"* and he got elephants to fly, God damn it!

Whether you think of yourself as a runner, a jogger, a plodder or a slogger, improving your speed is probably quite high up on your list of goals in terms of your running.

That and the perfect, flattering photo of you with flying feet (And we might be able to help you there too).

I know you are scared and possibly a little skeptical, but trust me, not being as fast as you would like and the confidence problems that come with that are probably the biggest things holding you back from truly enjoying the sport like you should.

All of that stops today as I unveil 7 simple ways to tackle your "Go Slow" mentality and get you running stronger and faster.

You CAN run faster, yes EVEN YOU. You just need to want it enough to make it happen. And keep the faith at ALL times.

Now go dig out those trainers. It's about to get messy around here.

The villains of this story

It takes a great deal of courage to stand up to your enemies,
but even more to stand up to your friends. — **J.K. Rowling**

Right ladies, before we get in to the HOW of improving your running speed we are going to spend just a little bit of time looking at the WHY and also the WHO, as we explore your reasons for running and meet some of the interesting characters in our life who sometimes negatively impact on our ability to improve.

So, WHY is improving our speed so important to us?

WHY do we find achieving improvements so incredibly difficult?

And WHY (just out of curiosity) is now the right time to finally tackle this head on?

WHO do we want to improve our speed for?

Whose opinion of our running do we care most about?

Let's take this back, way back.

Back to the beginning. Not the beginning of time, although that could be interesting.

But let's look at when you first took up running.

Because at first the goal was simply to be able to run, right? Remember that? Then it was simply to be able to run for more than five minutes without collapsing. Or was that just me?

Our WHYs might have read like this

- **For Weight loss**
- **To Improve Fitness**
- **To positively affect mood**
- **A New Challenge**
- **To fundraise for a good cause**
- **To meet new people**

Those WHY's got us started.

And for us to see some improvement we need to revisit that sense of WHY once more.

Try it. Make a list of 10 reasons why running faster would be great. Then sit for a few minutes and picture how it would feel to be a faster runner. Really picture it. Feel the good vibes, the energy your body would produce as you fly through the air.

We started from nothing and eventually managed to run for a sustained period of time using this WHY method, so it will work again. Trust me. But we have to first believe it is possible and not get in our own way.

Because back when we were progressing towards that all-important 5k distance, all the while there was this awful shadow hanging over this achievement, reminding us that regardless of all of this we were still not 'proper' runners.

"Yes I did the 5k, but I was so slow" we said.

"Oh yes I can run for 30 minutes without stopping, I'm just not very fast" we announced.

"I wouldn't say I am a runner, I jog. I just plod along really slowly, I could probably walk faster" we joked.

What the hell is our problem?

Why are we never happy?

If you move your legs more rapidly than a walk and there is an instant (no matter how small) in each step when both feet are off the ground, then I would suggest you are running.

What's with this unnecessary commentary on our own running speed?

What we are talking about here ladies is the completely useless, and sometimes uncontrollable manifestation of our own Self Doubt, AKA Villain #1 in our story.

I would go as far as saying in the running world this is the master of all the super evil Baddies, public enemy number one so to speak and the villain who shows up most often, causing us the most damage.

It's that nagging little voice which stops you from trying, that convinces you it's not worth it. That you are not worth it. It fills you with this insipid paranoia that convinces you that everyone is watching you, judging you, laughing at you.

Did you know in the UK 2 million fewer women than men play sport because of fear of being judged. How crappy is that? But I am on a mission to change that by getting 1 million overweight and inactive women running via my 'Too Fat to Run?' movement.

The only redeeming feature of villain #1 is that you can actually tame it yourself with a bit of positive self talk which of course takes practice, but it does do as it's told eventually. Tell it to 'Bog off!' often enough and it does get the message.

But more of that later (Or skip to Secret Weapon Number 2 IMMEDIATELY if you see this as your biggest downfall). For now though let's talk about our second type of baddie. I give you:

Villain #2: The Naysayer.

Sadly, the likelihood is these people are already quite close to you, they have infiltrated your world, have your trust, are around you all the time. They might even be your most dearest person, so you can't always escape these folk even once you have discovered them.

These critters get under your skin and habitually express negative and pessimistic opinions about your general choices in life, including your desire to run. They are quite clever baddies really as they have morphing superpowers and can appear in a range of interchangeable forms, each requiring their own dose of counteraction.

1. **The Jokers** – Are most likely to laugh when you announce you want to take up running, or rib you about your big bum in Lycra every time you put your kit on, under the guise of humour. They take the mickey out of all aspects of your new hobby with comments like "Yes Mum, Sue is off doing her Jogging thing."

2. **The Disbelievers** – Might be in denial about your hobby. They may pretend you don't do it at all or tell you flippantly that it's not even worth trying because you won't do it, you will give up like you always do, because it's too hard. They will use their own measure stick for what is possible, they may even use examples from their own running experiences. Like if I couldn't do it, you definitely won't, or maybe they're a better runner than you and simply don't want to see you improve.

3. **The Worriers** – These guys (actually they are most likely to be your Mum or Gran) are a bit like a full time risk assessor on a mission to get you to stop IMMEDIATELY. They will suddenly remember every ailment you have ever had, and every story of a runner being raped or dying of a heart

attack that was ever reported. But of course, they only have your own interest at heart. Or do they?

Be careful who you listen to, where you get your support from, and surround yourself as much as possible with other women who are at the same stage in running. Find yourself a safe place to discuss your goals and achievements without fear of judgment.

Villain #3 is The Heckler – These guys, and let's face it they are normally guys, are just dickheads. They serve no purpose other than to shame, annoy and anger us runners. They are possibly the villain we fear most, we hear such stories don't we? We expect them to be lurking in every shadow, ready to jump out at any given moment.

My first heckler story is a well-known one and it's how I got my nickname "Fatty Must Run". I was taking part in my first ever running event, a local 3K race. I had done no training and was at my largest, but I still wasn't expecting the abuse I received half way round.

"Run Fatty Run" came the call.

And from a snotty-nosed little kid in a Burberry cap.

I will never forget how that little shit made me feel, but I also have to thank him somehow for spurring me on to prove him wrong, to prove to everyone that you should be able to run at whatever size you are without fear of abuse.

I think with this one it's more the fear of being heckled rather than the reality of being abused which gives them their strength, because actually lots of women report that they have never been heckled.

The final antagonist and the one that is complained about the most on online forums and amongst the plus-sized running community more generally is.

Villain #4 The Running Snob - Of course these guys are the easiest of all of our antagonists to spot because they simply can't help themselves. Despite a strong desire to keep their elitist views underground, their provocative and always uncalled for comments seem to find a way of coming to the surface. And the topic of speed in particular brings out a special kind of reaction in them.

When someone asks if you drive you don't answer 'yes, but slowly'. The question is normally asked purely to ascertain whether a: you have the ability or skill to drive, and b: as to whether it is something you do often.

So why does the question "Do you Run?" often seem like such a loaded question?

Ultimately most people do not need to know your speed, but somehow we have got into this habit of apologizing for not being able to run at the pace that Olympic athletes can, or top club runners that consistently cover 20 or 30 miles a week.

We are runners. It is something we partake in, but it is not our job, it is not our vocation. On the whole running is something we do for enjoyment, for fitness and for wellbeing. Not to win prizes or accolades for speed.

But we continue to comment on our 'rubbish speed' and unfortunately so do other people.

When I was training for the London Marathon in 2012 I mentioned it to a local politician at a work function who enquired as to how long it would take me to get round the 26.2 mile course. Now having never run a marathon before, this was a complete guess.

And not wanting to be over ambitious I said, "I dunno, maybe 5 or 6 hours" to which he responded "Oh, so you are not a proper runner then?"

What a twat!

Only someone who has been involved in the sport of running at some point could make a comment like that...he was your typical Running Snob. Someone who wants to make you feel shit about your efforts, because they have a very clear idea of what a "Real Runner" is, based on an outdated concept of old school athletics...the world has moved on since Chariots of Fire people.

Because the average person is clueless about how far a marathon actually is, and even if they do know the distance they are unlikely to have any understanding of how long it takes a runner (of any ability) to run one.

This negative attitude of 'proper running' equaling speed is so damaging to the sport of running, but more importantly it can be devastating to the actual runners themselves. The mere mention of pace and an accompanying judgment on speed from complete strangers can absolutely knock your confidence.

Comments on social media are the worst. How many times do you see Jane from your running club post "Just come back from the worst run ever, 5K in 26 minutes! I can't believe how slow I am." Urrghhhh!

Now how helpful is that if you have spent the last year trying to get your time to under 35 minutes? I get that people want to express their disappointment at their own pace, but why not just say "not happy with my pace" or "a bit off my PB time" instead of making the link between an actual time and an assessment of whether that is a fast or slow pace?

In my opinion runners discuss speed with other runners for 3 reasons:

1. **To make you feel small because they know they can run faster**
2. **Because they are worried you are faster than them**
3. **To help them understand your current ability so as to help you improve or alternatively to ask your advice so they can improve**

I guess I am being a little harsh with the first two as I am sure, in the context of a friendly running club, the question of "How fast do you run a 5K?" or "How did you get on?" is asked out of curiosity and support more than an attempt to ridicule or belittle.

However, I have witnessed snobbery amongst some runners whereby if you can't meet a certain speed bracket for a 5k or 10k distance then you are not considered a real runner and that in turn dictates the behaviour and level of respect you are likely to receive.

A few years ago Jason Henderson, editor of UK running magazine "Athletics Weekly" made a comment on Twitter implying that joggers and plodders were in fact not 'real runners'. A subsequent blog post from me forced him to take the comment down and later he responded in a 2-page article that indeed confirmed his position; he believes that you do have to run at a certain speed to be considered a 'proper runner'.

Someone working in his position should know better than to fuel the massive gap between elite sport and recreational running, if not for any reason other than to encourage more people to get off their backside and exercise.

The thing is though, us slower runners make it easy for this discrimination to continue because we perpetuate that belief that you have to be able to cover a distance in a set time to be seen as a 'proper runner', because in truth we believe it too.

By constantly moaning about our slowness and using it as an excuse in training we back up the views that some faster runners have of us, so we can't really blame them.

If we ourselves are not positive about the fact we are running full stop, regardless of pace, how can we expect everyone else to see that as enough? Running as a sport has room for us all, that is what makes it such a great mass participation activity across the world.

So what are we to do?

If I made the rules up firstly I would put a stop to the use of the word SLOW altogether in the context of running. Because I don't think it actually serves any purpose other than to make people feel shit about themselves.

It's not like knowing you are slow motivates you to run any faster, because slow is relative and your slow could be the equivalent of someone else's fast, so the term is useless for any kind of comparative exercise or tool for improvement.

I have no problem with the word slower, because that tells us that a judgment is being made against another marker. So I may well be slower than Bob from running club, but I am faster than Mary from parkrun. Well most of the time anyway, and that kind of comparison can be useful. As is commenting that you were slower this week than last, or the first half of the marathon was slower than the second.

It is natural for us to make these types of assessments in our running. We like to know where we fit in the scheme of things, how we match up against others. It takes me back to being at school where a whole playtime could be taken up with a debate and practical assessment on who was the fastest boy and who was the fastest girl in the school. It's funny because this wasn't ever assessed in PE or even at the annual sports day. No, we knew who would win in structured races because we had spent all year hosting preliminary races checking often just in case the ranking had changed for some reason overnight.

The equivalent as an adult runner is your PB, your Personal Best or PR (Personal Record) as some people like to call it. When you have been running, and racing in particular, for a while you will start to become a bit obsessed with beating your previous times. And in the first few races as your fitness improves you may well do this. But then you start to get complacent, or you simply just can't run any faster for a number of reasons and that is when beating your PB becomes a bit of a quest.

In running clubs, or simply circles of runners, a common topic of conversation can be about PBs for different race distances and it is a useful way of talking about speed and your ambitions for improvement, particularly if you are coming back from injury or having a baby for example.

Knowing your ranking is helpful; knowing what you have to do to move up a place or how easy it would be to slip back down again can be motivating too.

Simply being labelled SLOW does not help at all.

SO STOP DOING IT.

While we are talking about things to stop doing can we please stop referring to the 'Tortoise and the Hare' fable? Us slower runners never, ever overtake the hare, we generally just run all by ourselves, and if not then with a whole heap of other frustrated tortoises.

And you know those info graphics on social media that read;

"I run, but I am slower than"

- **A turtle running through peanut butter**
- **Internet Explorer on dial up**
- **A plumber that charges by the hour**

Ok I made the last one up, but you get the point. They were funny the first time we heard them, but now that everyone has them on their Facebook page, or printed on bumper stickers and t-shirts, they have kind of lost their humour.

Let's stop poking fun at ourselves, let's stop inflicting unnecessary pain on others and let's stop apologising for our speed (or lack of it) and do something to improve it instead, or not if that's ok with you.

I have no problem with runners who take 60 minutes to run 5K. If you want to plod around, enjoying the scenery and making the most of your race entry, then why the hell not?

But some us really do feel the need for speed.

This chapter might seem a little negative, highlighting some of the things that are annoying about the sport of running, but it's worth noting that for every villain in this story there are hundreds of Superheroes out there restoring the balance of Good vs. Evil.

Complete strangers cheering you on, keeping you accountable, going out of their way to help with random acts of kindness. The running community can be magical, especially if you expect them to be. Amazing things happen when you consciously ignore the villains and seek out the Superheroes, like the chap in a suit who gave me an unexpected high five as I ran exhausted through a deserted shopping mall one night in Stratford.

I will never forget how that man made me feel. Just 5 seconds of kindness that will stick with me until the day I die. It reminds me of the Maya Angelou quote *"People will forget what you said, people will forget what you did, but people will never forget how you made them feel"*.

I have hundreds of stories like this. People who gave up their race to help others. Choosing exactly the right words to motivate. Hugs when you need them. And of course the sharing of jelly babies.

And the great thing is, once you have found your confidence as a runner you will find yourself being one of these Super-hero's too, and that is what we are going to work on next.

Finding your inner super hero

Above all, be the heroine of your life,
not the victim. - **Nora Ephron**

We haven't always been slow, have we ladies? Can you remember as children we never did anything slow, did we? If you had a chance to run you would take it, no questions asked.

We would zoom down corridors, dash across a field, scurry up the stairs; running slow simply wasn't an option back then.

When you watch toddlers who have just learned to walk, they take off and often get caught up in their own pace, unable to stop. It's only once they become steady on their little feet that they learn to control their speed a bit better, but they still push it at any given opportunity. Children are fearless and they simply have a need for speed. Well, until they turn into teenagers and then everything becomes an effort and is done at snail's pace.

Actually that's not completely true, even teenagers have their moments. Have you ever watched teenagers running away from the police?! Not that I would know myself, obviously...

When I was at secondary school it was about a 5-minute walk from our classroom block to the dinner hall for lunch, and we would always run to secure the best seats and best choice of grub. The school had a no running policy when moving around the school grounds and employed a little old lady to stand on the corner of the science labs calling out "No running girls, no running". Still to this day I can hear her strong Irish accent and I laugh at the fact that nobody ever listened to her, we just speed walked, like those people from the Olympics, until she was out of sight and then we started running again. We always arrived at the dinner hall red-faced and on a bit of a high. And that was before the cake and custard.

So let me take you back for a moment to that time as a child when you too ran like the wind.

Can you remember that incredible feeling of running so fast that falling over was inevitable, but we still didn't slow down did we?

Did we heck!

I often think about that feeling when I watch athletes in the 100-meter sprint when they cross the finish line and crash into the padded barriers at the opposite side of the stadium. They aren't holding back are they?

When I was about 11 my family were on a traditional British holiday, in a caravan, in Clacton-on-Sea. My younger sister Jennie and I had been sent to the camp shop to buy supplies and had been told by mum that we could spend the change for going. We got so excited that we literally sped off at 100 miles per hour through the rows of caravans to see what sweets we could buy.

My sister was naturally faster than me, but I wasn't going to let her beat me. I gave it all I had, which was clearly where it all went wrong. I can still remember the point where I realised I was going to fall over, knowing I was powerless to stop it. It kind of went in slow motion with me flying through the air and landing in the weirdest prayer-like position, acquiring huge grass stains on my new, white leggings and mud underneath my fingernails where I had tried without success to break my fall.

My sister thought it was the funniest thing and danced around my crumpled body with her legs crossed threatening to wet herself. To this day she reminds me of it. "Do you remember that time at the caravan where you praised the Lord?" and we both laugh uncontrollably!

If either of us took a tumble like that now I doubt it would be so funny. Well maybe it would be if it were my sister. But generally speaking as adults when we fall over and manage not to hurt ourself physically, it still kind of hurts psychologically. We are so much more conscious of our bodies now, and we would be mortified at being so completely out of control. How often have you taken a stumble and found your first thought to be "shit, I hope nobody saw that" rather than "oh no, have I hurt myself?"

The fact is, even now most of us could run fast if we really tried, but ultimately we are a tad lazy and simply petrified of falling over and making a fool of ourselves. In the case of an emergency for example all of those thoughts become secondary. When it is a life or death situation, perhaps involving a loved one, we would seriously pick up the pace to go and get help and somehow sustaining the increased level of energy output needed.

Do you know there is a marathon in Africa called "The Big 5" where you run across an African game reserve with the challenging marathon route going right through the habitat of the most famous African game: Elephant, Rhino, Buffalo, Lion and Leopard. No fences, no rivers, nothing at all separates the runners from the African wildlife. I wouldn't want to be the slowest in that field, would you?

So if we want to give you a compelling reason to run faster, being able to save your own life is not a bad one. Failing that having to run to save someone else's life is a pretty good motivator too.

I remember an incident my auntie told me about which happened to her when she was a nanny for two small children. She had taken the two children, aged around 4 years and 18 months to the forest for the day. They had toddled from the car into the forest for a couple of hours before the little boy became ill and started going all floppy and unresponsive. This was before the time of mobile phones. I can just imagine what was going through her brain; "how the hell do I get two small kids back to the car FAST?" But somehow she managed to carry both children and run back to the car park to get help.

Now my auntie is not a small woman and she is absolutely not a runner. But in an emergency, in a life or death situation you somehow just find the strength. Adrenaline starts flooding into the body and, more important than that, your sense of WHY is so strong, there is nothing that would stop you from getting to where you needed to be.

Another time as a child I saw yet another one of my quite large aunties running at speed during an emergency. We were at some seaside resort on the Kent coast about to go home after spending the day on the beach. As we were all piling back into the cars there was an almighty scream from my cousin. Her friend had managed to slip off the sea wall and had fallen 10 foot or so onto the sea bed. I had never seen an adult woman run as fast as she did...and she was in flip flops. My cousins friend was OK as she landed on soft mud...but I will never forget that sprint though.

Worryingly, outside of this "I only run when absolutely necessary" mentality, many of us have got into a mindset of speed equals effort and effort is somehow embarrassing for a fat person. Almost as embarrassing as falling over.

How many of us in every day life stop ourselves from running for a bus if it truly requires any level of pace? This is partly to do with laziness and a lack of fitness, but also to do with the possibility of missing the bus and feeling embarrassed about it, or have people on the bus laugh at the sight of your wobbly bits and red face as you try and catch it.

For many of us the fact we are out running at all is a bloody miracle, particularly when we have so many hang-ups with our bodies. But to add to that, I am now going to ask you to run faster too, OK?

Look ladies, let's just be straight:

- Faster requires **more movement**, movement equals wobble.
- Faster requires **more oxygen**, taking in oxygen means more heavy breathing, grunting even
- Faster requires **more effort**, effort means more sweat and redder faces

And people may laugh, especially if I fall over, and we all know that running at speed increases your chance of falling flat on your face. Yes, we are back to that again.

But go back to your WHY. Remember how awesome you will feel running a 5K just 5% faster. Not coming last every time. Getting closer to being able to run with friends.

Think about those athletes at the highest level of their sport, runners in the 100-meter sprint final in the Olympics for example. They are not worrying about looking stupid or falling over at the start line are they? As they prepare to give everything their body has in their quest for victory they are focusing solely on how it is going to feel having given it their all, win or lose.

So I guess we need to stop for a moment and ask do we REALLY want to get faster, do we REALLY want to progress, or are we simply hoping it will happen by some stroke of luck?

There is no doubt that running regularly improves fitness and speed, but only to a certain point. Heading out the door for your gentle jog around the neigbourhood twice a week for a year is great for maintaining a healthy lifestyle, but I doubt you will see much improvement in your speed. I would suggest that after 6 months or so, after you are able to run 5k without stopping you are likely to hit a plateau with your speed and that is when the frustration begins.

But as the saying goes;

"If you always do what you always did, you will always get what you always got."
Henry Ford

So it is easy my friend, you just need to run faster. And the best way to do that is, you guessed it, run faster. I am afraid that only you can make that happen, as unfortunately nobody else can do it for you.

Improving your speed is as simple as that; you just need to run faster. The moments in my running where I have seen marked improvements in my finish times were when I had given myself a real talking to half way round a course, or in the last few hundred metres. I would literally tell my legs to get a move on and when they did what I told them I saw results.

You might think that simply telling you to go out and run faster is unlikely to make much difference to your pace, but I stand by that uncomplicated sentiment, sometimes it really is as simple as that.

To get you into the habit of running faster I am going to introduce you to the seven different speed-inducing running techniques I have used this last year, helping me shave over 20 minutes off my 5k time.

Just imagine what difference running a 5k twenty minutes faster will make? Or ten minutes even? Actually, think for a moment about what knocking just a minute off your current time would mean to you right now:

- You might finally gain the confidence to join a running club
- You might enter a race
- You might find a running buddy
- You might run more frequently
- You might attempt larger distances because it won't take you so long

- You might even lose some weight or change in shape because of the increase in effort

I know that running fast is not the be all and end all in the sport of running, but it does open the door to further opportunities that a lack of pace sometimes prevents.

Often it is our unhelpful and negative attitude to our pace that is the barrier to progression and not the actual pace itself that is holding us back.

So how do you find your inner Super Hero?

The trick is to embody the ethos of your favourite superhero, your favourite athlete, or even just your favourite person.

Have you ever been in a bit of a sticky situation and thought:

"What would Beyonce do?"

Or

"I bet Anna from Frozen wouldn't put up with this shit"

The point is it doesn't matter who your role model is, it's just important you have someone to draw strength and inspiration from.

So come on, let's stop for a bit and think about who the best ever Super-hero's were and what they had in common:

- Wonder Woman
- Cat Woman
- Super Woman
- She-Ra
- Lara Croft

- Super Gran – Who remembers her?!

I asked the ladies in The Clubhouse who their go-to super heros were:

- The whole bunch of the new Ghostbusters women (right?)
- The mum from The Incredibles (Aha!)
- Storm from X Men
- My Mum, said one lady
- Katharine Hepburn said another
- Miss Piggy – because she's in a mixed species relationship, is a bit chubby and has succeeded in a male dominated environment

On my annual Too Fat to Run retreat in Greece each May, I ask my clients to identify a role model who they can channel when things are tough.

A young black girl who was with us got it immediately and said,

"Oh mine is Queen Latifa, I often think about what would she do with the things I have to face each day!"

I love rap artist turned movie star Queen Latifa too.

You see the point is, we are all inspired by different qualities and being able to channel those and locate them within yourself is critical.

So what do these ladies all have in common?

A 'can do' attitude? A recognisable look? A set of values?

Most of these characters have been constructed over time and we too can construct ourselves over time; we can choose to be whoever the hell we want to be, we can choose to be stronger, more powerful, more capable because chances are those qualities are there. They just need a little teasing out.

Now I am not asking you to wear a cape, red hot pants and knee high boots unless you really want to. But wearing the right running gear can feel like your armor, it can give you confidence and therefore a superpower that can help here. Perhaps it's one of the reasons you see so many female runners in tutus running the London Marathon.

A lovely lady from The Clubhouse once made a batch of superhero headbands and sold them as a way of raising money towards her Marathon Fundraising goal. I still wear mine now. It has the words POW!, Krunch and the like all over it and is in bold bright colours. I always feel badass when I wear it!

"You're much stronger than you think you are, trust me" said superman. Funnily enough I couldn't find a single quote from Super Woman on the internet, just lots of sexy images. Urgh it's a fix, I tell ya.

But let's not get angry, let's get even.

So we need to make up our own subtitles, our own commentary, our own inspirational memes about our role as superwomen in this world, because we all know that Hero's are made by the paths that they choose, not the powers they are given.

You may worry that all eyes are on you when you head out for a run, or even when you are simply talking about your running stuff but who knows what lives you are changing while you are out there doing your thing.

Inspiration comes in all shapes and sizes and who are you to deny your neighbours, friends and family that? We seriously have some work to do to collectively change the status quo in running, to normalize sport for women who are not traditionally sporty.

Every time you lace up your trainers and head out in public you are challenging perceptions. That in itself deserves a medal in my eyes.

I bet you are already a superhero in many people's eyes, but you just don't realise it.
Now is the time to start seeing and embracing your true power, and to start believing in yourself.

Attitude is everything.

Now get out there and kick some ass!

The mission, if you should accept

I do not try to dance better than anyone else.
*I only try to dance better than myself – **Arianna Huffington***

Time to put this theory into action right?

We have established that for us to have meaningful conversations about our progress in running then we are all going to have to stop talking about SLOW. Instead we need to start talking confidently about our current capabilities in terms of pace and speed.

And a good starting point for this is to start thinking a bit about what your goals are for the 60-day challenge you are about to embark on. How fast do you really want to go?

What should my goal look like?

Remember Speed is relative and your goals need to be too.

"I would like to run faster" is more of a dream or an ambition than a goal, so we need a bit of specificity, pin down exactly how much time you would like to knock off. Be realistic, but ambitious too.

5%, 10%, 20% off?

Or 3 minutes, 4 minutes or 5 minutes off?

Maybe it's to dip under a specific time goal? Like a sub 30 minute 5K

It is your goal so express it however you chose.

Once you know your goal, write it down somewhere visible in big, squiggly, bright text. Own it. Talk about it frequently. Speak as though it is already in the bag with "When" language rather than

"If" language and most importantly don't let anyone convince you that your goal is not important or viable.

What else do I need to understand to help me with all of this?

As a newish runner you may be a little overwhelmed by the language and terminology used in discussions about speed and in some cases it may actually be the mathematics of it all that baffles you.

That is most definitely my problem.

I have never been good at numbers; I failed my GCSE Maths twice at school and struggle on a daily basis to do even the simplest of equations. In fact, anything to do with figures gets me all in a fluster and this fear has seriously impacted on my running. For many years I have stuck my head in the sand when it comes to my pace and just run.

The only time I cared about was my finishing time, but of course by that point the run was finished and the end result final. My serious lack of comprehension when it comes to pace and speed is a huge factor when it comes to my assessment of what has held me back from ever seeing any real improvement all these years.

So what is the difference between pace and speed?

Not a lot really...

Pace - Is the measurement of speed, i.e. how it is recorded in the moment as it happens. In talking about your pace to others you might talk about running at an average 16-minute mile pace, or a 7-minute per kilometre pace for example.

Speed – Is the rate at which a person or object covers a distance, so is more like the end result. So this is where your 5 miles per hour thinking comes into play. Which coincidently is roughly my speed give or take a few minutes.

So basically it is two different ways of explaining the very same thing; how fast you are running. I personally prefer to talk in terms of pace because it is a little easier for me to work out how quickly I can cover a set distance, rather than how many miles I can cover in a set time.

Should I measure in miles or kilometres?

I guess much of this depends on whether you work in metric or imperial, or what distances you are running. I rely on my Garmin now to tell me my current speed and pace, eliminating the need for any mathematics. I just have to remind myself to set it to miles or kilometres depending on the race I am training for.

For example, when training for a 10k race I would set it to count kilometres, but if training for a marathon I would use miles to get me to the 26.2 goal. But it doesn't really matter for our purposes here, just choose one and be consistent across the 60 days.

What distance should I be concentrating on?

I run marathons, I run them reasonably slow in the whole scheme of things. In fact I worked out the other day that Paula Radcliffe runs her marathons 3 times faster than me, but I am 4 times fatter so technically speaking that makes me the better runner, right?

But look, there is no point in focusing on your speed if you are unable to run consistently over a set distance or timeframe. By that I mean completing a 5k running constantly, or being able to run without stopping for 30 minutes or so.

Consistent, steady running is really important when you want to increase your speed. You need a baseline level of fitness to give you the confidence to know you can complete the set distance regardless of how hard you have to push.

You may have a particular distance in mind that you want to improve your time over, maybe a 10K or a half marathon. The 7 techniques that follow will help you do this, however if it is an improved marathon time you are after there are probably more technical books out there on the market. You will see improvements from using the tips in this book, but as with any long distance training you will need to integrate these speed sessions into your longer term plan which can be challenging and not something I make reference to.

In my research for this book I focused on the shorter 5K distance because it meant I didn't need to commit an awful lot of time on my training sessions, and I could test it with more women but the long term goal for me was to improve both my 10K and half marathon times simply by learning how to run faster.

Whichever distance you decide to focus on is fine with me, just make your choice and stick to it.

How should I be measuring and recording my improvements?

Over the years I have used different gadgets to record my race times and training pace improvements, of which there were few in the early years. I only really saw any improvement once I bit the bullet and bought myself a proper running watch. This was for the following reasons:

- It marked a significant moment in my life where I started to take my running seriously
- It was a big financial outlay for me so I was determined to get my money's worth

- The ability to scrutinise not only finishing times, but average times and lap breakdowns in detail taught me to look for patterns
- Being able to actually adjust my running speed in real time as a result of the continual reading of my running stats in a race or in training

So is a Sports Watch worth getting?

In my opinion, yes. It forces you to really come to terms with your pace and to recognise your potential to improve if you are willing to work at it. And owning a Garmin made me feel like a real runner, so in the end I had to start acting like one too.

If you can't or don't want to buy one, then a decent stop watch and a recording system will work, particularly if you have decent arithmetic skills to work out timing on the go. A stopwatch doesn't tell you distances so you may also need to measure your routes in advance to help with your calculations.

But remember, there are a whole heap of mobile phone apps available for free that can do a lot of this for you. Nike+, RunKeeper and MapMyRun are just a few examples so you can get by without an all singing, all dancing gadget.

But gadgets do not make you run faster, YOU make yourself run faster. Sports watches, phone apps and other flashy bits of new technology may just help you along the way. My advice in terms of gadgets is to test a few systems out first to find one that works for you before embarking on your 60-day challenge.

Right, you ready to get started? Well what are we waiting for!

Let me introduce you to the 60-day challenge:

1. You need to set aside 60 days to test the 7 techniques. Print out our 12-week planner from our free resource page and schedule some time to set and record your baseline. Plan seven weeks of hardcore training and then a small gap (to rest your legs) before testing your improvement in a final dash.

2. Choose a specific improvement goal, work out what 5%, 10% and 20% faster would look like for you, and more importantly how achieving this goal would make you feel.

3. You want to consistently be running 3 times a week. You can still incorporate any regular running you do with a structured group and it gives you the flexibility to add the occasional longer run or recovery run if you need it. If you seriously doubt you can manage 3 runs a week check out Secret Weapon #1 which might be a helpful alternative

4. Take each Scream Technique in turn, but as you progress through the weeks keep in mind the previous techniques and incorporate them accumulatively into your running.

5. Each week you will be expected to take part in a time trial to measure improvements. This is key so schedule this in. Testing your speed regularly in race conditions is THE best way of making steady improvements in pace.

Why the time trials?

Often people complain to me that they never seem to get faster. When I ask them how frequently they race, they say 'never', or so infrequently it doesn't make much of an impact on their times.

When you know your time is being measured and recorded by someone else it seems to matter so much more how fast you cover the distance. Add to that the effect of running with others in a so-called race and you tend to up your game a bit due to your embedded competitive spirit. Yes, we all have it somewhere deep inside.

For years I ran with something called the "shame factor" which basically meant if people were watching me I would force myself to run stronger in an effort to not feel so ashamed. I now know that the word shame is not a helpful one; why should I feel ashamed for walking or running slowly if that is all I can do at that point? Instead of helping me to improve as a runner what this sense of shame did was encourage me to stop/start more and look for excuses to stop running as often as I could. I would give it all I had while in public view and then as soon as I was in a quieter location I would feel like I had earned the right to walk or jog.

I have since turned this on it's head and I now prefer to call this phenomenon my "runner's pride", so when I have an audience I hold my head up high and run as consistently as I can manage at that given time. If I am feeling really strong or there is someone I really want to impress, then that is when I really pick things up. But most importantly in those moments when I don't have anyone watching I do it for myself, I do it so that I can be impressed by my ability and determination to carry on. This has resulted in me becoming a much more consistent runner and a runner in control of my own effort levels.

If you are one of those people that feel embarrassed about your pace, or your form, or your body shape or anything else you can think of, then you should definitely sign up immediately to a weekly time trial.

If you are lucky enough to have one near you, sign up to parkrun, a FREE weekly 5K time trial, which is taking the UK and the rest of the world by storm with over 1 million registered runners. The premise is simple; you turn up at 9am every Saturday morning, you run your 5k with a few hundred other runners and a little later that day you get sent your time which also sits on a public website for everyone else to see.

Now if that doesn't motivate you to improve your time week on week then I don't know what will. Remember, it is not just the idea of being accountable that helps you to speed up, the process of running the same route regularly can also help you to set goals.

To find out more about parkrun and how it all works check out www.parkrun.com

When I first started running at my local parkrun at Wanstead Flats in East London I could only run to the first wooded bit before needing to walk. Gradually I increased it until I could run the first lap, then the first lap and up to the trees and then of course to the point where I could run the whole 5K without the need to stop at all.

Now that I can complete the course I rarely think about walking anymore because I have the confidence in my fitness to get me round. I use certain bits of the route to speed up, like the start trying to keep up with the crowd for as long as possible, or battling up the hilly bit and running strong on the downhill bits. The more you know a course the more confidence you have to push yourself around it.

At something like parkrun you are also likely to be running against the same runners weekly, so you get to understand where you fit in the pecking order running with the same runner in front of you and the same runners behind you. This gives you a target for improvement and of course they will be doing the same so you constantly have someone to compete and compare against.

You can even compete against the fastest runners too if it is a looped course which many of them are. When I first started I used to get overtaken by the finisher about 800 metres before I had done my first lap, now I pretty much always finish my first lap before the winner comes through. It's small things like that which motivate me to get a shifty on when I am feeling lazy or tired.

If you are still not convinced about committing to something as structured as parkrun then you can do a time trial in other ways too.

- **Find a timekeeper** - You could recruit a friend to act as timekeeper each week whilst running a familiar 5K route The pressure of having someone waiting for you and assessing your times could act as a very effective motivator. Try and do this at the same time of day on the same route so as to limit the variables

- **Treadmill** – A great way of testing your speed is by running on a treadmill, because at least with a treadmill you can adjust the speed manually and you have technology to help illustrate your pace and how far you have run. Treadmill running is not for everyone though and doesn't have the social aspects of healthy competition, but it is a useful tool to have for when you really can't run outside, or are travelling etc.

- **OneBigFatRun** - This is a monthly time trial with a difference. It is a virtual race that I coordinate via my Facebook community (www.facebook.com/thefatgirlsguidetorunning).The idea is to run your 5K and to upload your time to the page.

So as part of this 60-day challenge I recommend you to do a time trial on the same course as often as you can, with a final one scheduled right at the end to review your marked improvement. The idea though is not necessarily to go hell for leather each week, but instead to take this time to focus on the implementation of some of the other techniques within this book.

You may see your times going down weekly, but equally you may not, especially if you are doing hill work, or are just a bit fatigued. But please keep the faith, as each week you will be building in strength and learning about your capabilities in a friendly and reasonably controlled setting. If you are going to get a PB anywhere it is on a course you know and love, surrounded by people that love and respect what you are trying to do.

What if I am already doing this?

It is quite possible that you already do parkrun or a time trial of some sort and haven't seen much improvement, or perhaps you saw improvement when you first started, but now you have plateaued. This is probably because you just turn up each week and don't really have a plan. By introducing some of the other techniques into this weekly run you will smash your current PB in no time.

One of the biggest crimes in running when you are trying to achieve a specific goal is simply heading out the door without a plan. As I explained before, you can run regularly for years and years but if you always run the same routes using the same amount of effort you are unlikely to ever see any significant improvements.

Have you got your goal?

Are you good to go?

Great.

Preparing for battle

Courage is like a muscle. We strengthen it by use - **Ruth Gordo**

The act of buying this book and reading this far tells me you are committed to your desire to run faster and therefore you need to do whatever it takes to see that desired improvement come into fruition.

And that means taking action.

That means making a plan and acting upon it.

It means running.

It means running when it's difficult to run.

It means pushing your body harder than you might want it to.

So let's talk about how you prepare for this challenge to give you the best odds of completing it.

Firstly, choose a time to start when you are most likely to do this thing properly. Talk it through with loved ones, involve them if you must, but do not let outside factors get in the way of you achieving your goal. Remember villains can be found in the unlikeliest of places.

You will have to keep records

I find the best way is not using flashy technology, online diaries or gadgets, but instead on good old-fashioned paper pinned somewhere visible so you can look at it. There is something about writing your results down using pen and paper, so remember to download and print out the FREE 12-week planner, 60 day

programme prompt and record sheet from
www.toofattorun.co.uk/freeresources

The programme is meant to be flexible and of your own personal choosing, so my suggestion is to read through the techniques and then sit down with your diary to pencil in which sessions you are going to do and when. Of course these can change if need be, but seeing your sessions laid out and committed to on paper will make you more inclined to stick to them.

Set yourself a baseline

You will need a 5K baseline. A run with a well thought-out route and race conditions are going to give you a more realistic baseline time to work with than a meander around your local area with your watch giving you a rough time.

This baseline should be run at full pelt, as hard as you can possibly run. Otherwise you are seriously cheating yourself. You want to see real improvement right? Even if it's only you that knows the difference, trust me that cheating mentality will play on your mind. Go full out.

Now, let's talk about accountability

I know that if I don't have someone or something keeping me accountable my running suffers. I realised pretty early on in my blogging career, if I didn't run I didn't have anything to write about.

Later I realised the importance of having a community of runners who are at a similar level to you. A safe space, a space where people are willing you to do well. Supporting you when things don't go to plan.

Have some fun on Instagram, Twitter and Facebook using the following hashtags;

#TFTRscream
#TFTRSpeed
#Faster5K #
TooFattoRun

Let people know you have read this book and are currently following the programme, share what your current 5K speed is and what your improvement goal is. You could even post a picture of your tracking document as this will help with accountability.

The benefit of doing this with others

Why not try doing this programme with a running buddy, real or virtual? Things are always easier when you don't have to do them alone. Especially if you find yourself procrastinating or without the willpower to go it alone, if you struggle to find someone locally why not think about joining one of my 'Scream if You want to Go Faster' online programmes?

We follow the very same techniques, but I set you goals and targets, team you up with accountability buddies, send you pep talk videos and of course you get a closed Facebook group to share all your progress on. Look in the back of this book for a discount code to use against any of our online programs.

In the pilot phase we didn't set up a separate Facebook group, so what we noticed was the women who were part of The Clubhouse, our online running club, were more successful in getting their 3 runs done each week, and stuck at the programme longer than those that went it alone.

A number of participants paired up with friends locally; they did particularly well too. There are lots of benefits of running with others, which we will explore later in the book.

Remember to capture your progress

Why not take a picture of your sports watch at the end of your baseline and then again at the end of your final run. Seeing the two times side by side would be truly inspirational for other women starting out on this journey.

Alternatively, why not just write your improvement on a piece of paper (like 4 minutes etc.) hold it in front of you and get someone to take a photograph so that we can see the huge smile on your face too.

Remember to share these on social media. I would love to see your progress.

So, we are almost ready, bar the required health and safety check up.

Make sure you are in good health before embarking on this 60 day challenge

- Visit your Doctor for a check up
- Make sure you have decent trainers
- Listen to your body - if it really hurts STOP
- Be sensible when it comes to personal safety

Right, enough of the boring stuff, finally we are ready to begin.

Scream 1 – Have a little word with your legs

A lot of people are afraid to say what they want.
*That's why they don't get what they want - **Madonna***

So hopefully you all have your baselines done and recorded somewhere (you can find a FREE downloadable record sheet here), and so we begin with the easiest and most effective of our techniques...one which requires your brain to do most of the work rather than your body.

Let me explain.

Chances are many of you already ran faster during the baseline run than you thought you might simply because you knew you would have to record it somewhere, illustrating just how powerful our thoughts are in motivating us.

Earlier we talked about the voices in our head. Villain #1. The voice that often sounds like this;

- Who do I think I am?
- What's the point, I'm rubbish
- Everyone will look at me/laugh at me
- I'm too old/fat/tall/small/dumb/smart/poor/rich etc. for all of this.

The great thing with your mind though is you can tell it to shut up. Especially once you have realised what a pain in the arse it is.

You can turn things round 100% by using that powerful muscle for good.

I can't remember when exactly I started using this technique, but whenever I think to use it while out running it always works. The trick is to commit to it and believe in it 100%. If you put it down to psychological mumbo jumbo then you are already admitting defeat.

A good example of this is when I was asked by a PR company earlier this year to go on a press trip to run the Geneva Half Marathon. The other bloggers and journalists who came out were all super fit and super fast, I was the token normal person, which was fine.

The Geneva Half Marathon takes place amongst a whole weekend of running events, with races at every distance. I found out the day before the half there was a 10K women only race, and I was like, "Oh I want to do this too" so I did and it was fab. I got a reasonable time and finished middle of the pack somewhere. There were lots of newcomers to the sport, women of all shapes and sizes and it gave me a lot of confidence for the following day.

That didn't last long the following morning as I scanned the crowd for another fat person. I found one, a Yorkshire man who had set himself a challenge to run 50 European half marathons in his 50th year. He recongnised me from my blog and we talked for a bit in the starting area.

He was fat, but boy was he fast! He left me for dust in the first few minutes of the race.

I started off at the pace I always do for a half marathon; about 11 or 12 minute miles and a few minutes in I realised I was in last position. Like, seriously? You have got to be kidding me!

The sweeper van was traveling at ten miles an hour with its hazard lights and a really annoying beeping siren, travelling so slow it was struggling not to stall.

All kind of things went through my mind in that moment:

Should I just give up now?

I can't take that bloody siren for 13 more miles
How bloody embarrassing

With the official Geneva Running Festival T-shirts sporting the provocative slogan "Fast is Beautiful" I couldn't help but laugh at what a pickle I was in.

And then something switched in me. The scenery was beautiful, the conditions were perfect and I did not want to be accompanying the sweeper van for the duration of this race.

I spotted a lady ahead of me, focused on her, told myself I could catch her and I did. Then I focused on a small group of youngsters laughing their way around the course, not taking it too seriously; I could get them too.

And so it went on. I stopped counting at about 35 people. The point was I escaped the sweeper vehicle because I knew psychologically I would not be able to cope with that for the whole race. I also had a good talking to myself and knew I could run 10-minute miles if I really wanted to.

I had been flown all the way to Switzerland for this race and I sure as hell wasn't going to come last, even if it would make for a good story for a future blog or book. Apparently 50% of runners beat their PB on this course. My PB at the time was 2.27 for a half, but that was about 7 years ago before becoming a mum.

Even with sore legs from the previous night's race, hardly any crowds on the roads (they had all gone once the faster runners had passed) I managed to keep motivated and run strong, in what turned out to be one of the hottest spring days in history.

I was in the last 0.5% of the field, and at one point there was a lovely downhill section that seemed to go on for miles. The roads were empty apart from a line of cones dividing up the lanes, and there were hardly any spectators at this point. For a moment I thought "This is what Paula Radcliffe must feel like when she's leading the pack".

A girl can dream, right?

Throughout the race, but especially when things got tough I kept telling my legs they were strong and that I could do this. Sometimes this was in my head, and sometimes it slipped out and I could be heard saying "come on Julie, come on" out loud for all to hear.

I finished in 3 hours 11 minutes and 11 seconds. By no way a PB, but 5 minutes into the race it was looking like it might be a DNF (Did not finish)

And all through the power of the mind.

So, what is this week's challenge?

This week I want you to think yourself faster.

In its most basic form this is about willing yourself to up your speed.

My actual technique is to tell my legs to run faster.

YES.

I actually talk to my legs.

Sometimes this is in my head and sometimes it's actually out loud, especially if nobody is in earshot. Which is often, because often most people are well ahead of me.

Below are 3 techniques you may wish to try as part of your 3 runs this week; remember one of these must be a 5K run as fast as you can.

1. Create a GO FASTER mantra

Grab a piece of paper and write a short mantra that you can memorise and repeat over and over again. Fill it with positive affirmations about being stronger, faster and more capable. Eliminate any thoughts of being SLOW (in fact avoid using that word altogether for the next 7 weeks). When you are out running repeat your mantra as often as you need to.

2. Run FASTER every few minutes

This is otherwise known as interval training, and a useful way to test your speed for short bursts. Try it for 30 seconds every 3 or 4 minutes, or do two minutes fast two minutes slow for as long as you can last.

3. Give your legs a GOOD talking to

Go on you know you want to try this one. Whenever you are out running and you feel your legs are slacking, shuffling or taking it easy, focus all your attention on them and tell them to get a move on. Think about how it feels to be in control of how they move. Don't let them be the boss of you, you have the power to make them go faster, so remind them who is boss once and for all.

So just to recap the challenge this week is simple; it's 3 runs, one of which must be a 5K to test improvements against your baseline. The task is to trick your body into moving faster with nothing more than the will of the mind to do it. Trust me, your body will do as it's told and follow you wherever you take it.

Give it a go, what have you got to lose? Other than a few minutes off your 5K time.

Getting your 3 runs in this week is key, so don't go too mad on run #1 to the point where you can barely move the following days. Pace yourself, and then really go for it on your time trial towards the end of the week.

In the pilot, this technique was the 2nd most effective of the 7, but the one that women said they kept coming back to throughout.

The participants all experienced improvements in their 5k times in week 1, but more importantly they reported back that this more positive attitude had a profound effect on their confidence, and their enjoyment of running.

Especially the mantras they created for themselves,

"I still use my mantra. In fact, it has since got me 3 new PBs at parkrun," said one rather proud lady in the programmes feedback.

My mantra in case you were wondering is:

"You are strong, you are powerful, this is easy. You have got this in the bag." And trust me, it works for me.

Spend some time creating your mantra, your positive affirmation. Keep it short and memorable using the words you want to be like, not the words you don't. So "Don't be slow, don't be slow" will not work but "I am strong, I am swift" might.

Once you have it, stick it somewhere visible as a daily reminder. It might even rub off in different areas of your life.

Some people find talking to their reflection in a mirror helps. This technique was developed by self-help guru, Louise Hay, who says:

"Mirror work is the most effective method I've found for learning to love yourself and see the world as a safe and loving place."

Basically, it is the process of saying positive affirmations to your own reflection in the mirror. It is an odd thing to do at first, but with practice you feel less and less stupid, and it is incredibly powerful. Louise says this is because:

"The mirror reflects back to you the feelings you have about yourself. It makes you immediately aware of where you are resisting and where you are open and flowing. It clearly shows you what thoughts you will need to change if you want to have a joyous, fulfilling life".

If you feel a bit silly or self conscious working on yourself in this way just remember so many huge sporting champions have mindset coaches and deploy strategies to visualise their success, and will have mantras that they repeat over and over again throughout training and sometimes while competing.

Start listening to the intimate soundtrack of your mind, the constant and sometimes unconscious stream of messages you transmit to and about yourself and your abilities in life. Tuning in is step one; step two is broadcasting the message you actually want to hear.

Tennis sensation Billy King said;

"Self-awareness is probably the most important thing towards being a champion."

And she is so right.

OK so we are not aiming necessarily to win our races, but we do want to be the best versions of ourselves, right? That old adage of "as long as you do your best" is so fitting even now as adults, yet so often we beat ourselves up and are super critical of our progress, rather than celebrating our successes.

A lovely positivity coach I know called Pam Burrows ran a marvelous webinar session with our Clubhouse members one month about exactly this topic, and she used the visual prop of an inflatable mallet to illustrate how often we punish ourselves with negative messages. It was funny to watch at the time, but super powerful as it illustrated how inappropriate it is to treat ourselves in that way.

So every time you hear a negative thought come into your head, I want to you visualize yourself being hit over the head with a mallet. And instead replace that thought with a more positive one. Over time you will see how this might change the way you think about yourself and your capabilities as a runner.

Right ladies.

I want you to go out there this week and really compete with yourself, and let me know how you get on with "Having a word with your legs" by posting your progress on social media using hashtags #TFTRScream or #TFTRSpeed

If things get really tough and you feel like taking it out on someone, you can always use a tongue in cheek hashtag my Clubhouse ladies love using on social media:

#Iblamejulie

Scream 2 - Become a little more streamlined

*To all the women who think they are fat because they are not a size zero, you are beautiful, society is the ugly one - **Marilyn Monroe***

Over the years there has been so much research into why the Africans are so powerful in long distance running, but as a mere spectator it doesn't take too much scientific knowledge to simply look at any professional runners' physique, African or not, to see why the average recreational runner is at a serious disadvantage. And us fat runners even more so.

I am of course talking about body mass.

Individuals with perfectly conditioned bodies are suitable for the sport of running; those of us carrying around the equivalent of another runner in excess weight are not. Apparently.

Now I am not for a minute saying that slim equals fast and large equals slow in the running world, because being slim or even athletic-looking does not guarantee that you will be a really fast runner. However, the laws of gravity, energy and movement means at least they have the potential to run fast given some training.

It stands to reason doesn't it? The larger you are the more weight you have to unceremoniously cart around your race distance, therefore requiring greater energy consumption from the runner in question. There is probably a clever formula somewhere for extra energy requirements per pound of body weight. Why do you think they get army recruits to train with packs on their backs?

It's funny, in 2014 when I ran the Brighton Marathon I had a guy running in front of me with a huge backpack wearing army fatigues. He was really struggling in the heat with the extra load and someone in the crowd asked how much he was carrying, to which he responded "30lbs". Well that is about the amount of weight I still have to lose to get to goal weight, so I could feel his pain. I mean I do every time I go for a run. I guess we don't ever look at it like that though do we?

So do I need to go on a diet?

This chapter is not about fat shaming you into going on a strict diet so that you can play with the big boys, but it is about you coming to terms with the possibility that your weight is one of the contributing factors to your current speed limitation.

Losing bodyweight is an option though, isn't it?

It is at least something you potentially have some amount of control over. Within a 4-6 week period you could probably lose about 5% of your body weight without too much difficulty, but it would require you to follow a strict regime eliminating some foods you enjoy and going to some effort around portion control and the right mix of protein, fats and carbs.

Or would it?

Often when you up the amount of training you are doing, like when you really are pushing yourself at every session, you find that you will lose some weight initially or perhaps simply tone up without actually changing your diet much at all. However, you can't out-train a bad diet, so have an honest word with yourself about this and just be careful not to overcompensate for your extra exercise by overindulging in the foods you know won't help you reach your goal.

If becoming smaller is one of your goals, be comforted by the fact that as your body fat goes down and your body muscle and fitness goes up, your times should automatically come down. But ONLY if you continue to push hard every time you run.

Having less weight to carry round will require less energy than before, leaving you with more energy to focus on speed and technique. Your smaller frame will also make you more aerodynamic and light through the air with less resistance to the elements, like wind for example, allowing you to run super fast.

Each year I lead a 'Too Fat to Run?' Retreat in Rhodes, Greece, and last year there was a marvelous lady called Jo who came along. She has been a Clubhouse member right from the start and is one of the most confident, smart and go-getting women I have ever met.

She also happens to be gorgeous, inside and out. She oozes confidence and sex appeal and has a great attitude towards her body.

Throughout the week as we started digging deeper into the ladies' issues with body confidence and wider health, Jo admitted she did want to slim down for health reasons and by the end of the week she said this corker;

"Initially I started running to lose weight, now I want to lose weight to become a better runner".

So before you start this experiment you need to ask yourself if weight loss is something you want to focus on. I know my running speed would improve if only I was to lose the final two stone I need to lose, but if I am being honest I have never managed to get my eating right whilst training. I find that when I focus on my eating too much I get mega stressed and end up going completely off track. I am focusing on my running at the moment, so as long as I am not gaining weight, then I am happy.

Please note. This is no easy task. As outlined by many of our ladies, it was the week of the programme where lots of participants simply held their hands up and said;

"Sorry, didn't do this"

And responses like this one;

"I struggle with this one. I think it's really difficult to fuel for a run especially when I always seem to be on a diet. Getting the balance between having enough fuel to run and the desire to eat less to lose weight is my biggest struggle"

I hear you sister!

This is not something you are going to crack over night, but it is still worth considering.

But, is it possible then to do this without losing any weight at all?

Absolutely!

How often have you stood at the start of a race and seen the front-runners stripping off to the point where they are almost naked? This is not because they want to taunt you with their perfectly toned bodies. It's because they understand that the fewer clothes they have on the lighter and more aerodynamic they are and the less chance there is of having a wardrobe malfunction of any type.

In contrast, when you look at the back end of a marathon, many runners look like they are about to embark on a 10-day hike. Backpacks, windbreakers tied round waists, water bottles, bum bags, food supplies. I mean, this is a race not a flipping picnic!

If you are running for less than 10 kilometres or for about an hour you require your body, a pair of running shoes and some clothes to maintain your modesty. Nothing more and nothing less. I often run even further than this without the need for any other stuff, but I know some people feel naked or vulnerable without certain so-called essential items.

Every additional item that you add to your running kit not only adds weight and bulk to your run, but it also gives you something else to fuss over or stress about before, during and after the run.

A multimillion-pound industry has been created around running kit and the advertising world and other runners themselves do a great job in making you think you need it all.

YOU DON'T.

We fuss about so many things when we go for a run making it far more complicated than it needs to be.

- **I might get cold**
- **It might rain**
- **I need music to motivate me**
- **I want to measure my distance**
- **I need somewhere to store my keys and purse**
- **What if I have an accident and need to call home?**
- **What if the sun gets in my eyes?**
- **I get thirsty when I run**
- **My lips sometimes get dry**
- **I get hungry by about mile 4**
- **I like to carry mints**
- **I don't like my bum showing**
- **I want to take pictures**

Seriously guys, if you want to improve your times then dump all this stuff and become as streamlined as possible. You want to get to the point where you only ever run in kit that is absolutely perfect for you and kit that is absolutely necessary for your specific run. If you want to run with music fine, if you like running with a Garmin watch then cool, your keys and phone need to go somewhere, but do you seriously need a belt thingy to hold them, or could your back pocket do the job?

Over the years I have learned some vital tips and tricks that make me more streamlined without ever having to lose a single pound:

- Buy a small karabiner to attach to your keys. This can then clip to your waist or bra straps meaning your keys won't jiggle in a pocket. You could always get a single key cut to take with you running, leaving your bigger set at home, or in the car at a race.

- A well-fitting supportive bra with the straps adjusted properly can help you shave minutes off your time. Not having to worry about your boobs going AWOL and having the confidence to really go for it without knocking yourself out is invaluable.

- Do not put your phone down your bra ladies. Not only can the sweat damage your phone, but this has also been linked to Breast Cancer. A sock or wrapping your phone in cling film can keep it dry and prevent you from getting it out to make a call or take pictures during a race.

- If you really need water on your training runs, choose routes where you know there are water stops on the way allowing you to leave your bottles at home. You will run faster if you have both arms free to allow for good technique. If worst comes to worst, you can always knock on someone's door and ask for a glass of water.

- Clothes tied around your waist make you look bigger than you are and usually tend to be uncomfortable too. If there is any chance of you stripping off a layer in the first 10 minutes, do it before you leave home, or at the very start of a race.

- Always wear one layer less than you think you need. If you are cold you are more likely to get a move on to keep warm, if you are too hot you are less likely to want to push on.

- A simple well fitting pair of running tights (3 quarter length work best for me) will be the single best investment after your sports bra and running shoes. Running skirts, shorts, jogging pants etc. will slow you down and make you more self-conscious.

- Always buy running trousers with drawstrings at the waist. This gives you greater control allowing you to tighten them or loosen them from week to week. Check they are done up tight enough each time before setting off. There is nothing worse than having to constantly pull up your trousers or stopping to retie them.

- Gloves and a hat can work wonders to warm you up when wearing a race vest, and can be shoved in your bra or waistband when no longer needed. But don't take them if you don't really need them.

- Sort your hair out. If you have to stop every few minutes to retie your hair, or push your hair out of your eyes you will be distracted. Use a hair band, hat or one of our fabulous 'Too Fat to Run?' Head Buffs to keep it under control.

- Check your shoes are not weighing you down. Make sure you have the best shoes you can afford, shoes that are right for your feet and shoes that are going to support your running style. You will not believe the difference a good pair of running shoes can make to your pace. And PLEASE tie your laces well before you head out. Double tie them so the chance of them coming undone is impossible.

- If you must use music make sure you sort your playlists before you go and have headphones which give you the option to skip easily, nothing worse than trying to change music manually while you run, or having to listen to uninspiring music. And remember that not being able to hear what's going on around you is not very smart.

Being confident in your kit will allow you to focus completely on your running. But if you are overweight this isn't always as simple as it sounds. Finding technical kit that fits if you are anything over a UK size 16 is tough, and even if you can find kit in your size the chances of you feeling 100% confident in it are reasonably slim, as we are a fussy lot. This is something us fatties have to get over, we simply need to find the best kit we can and grow to love it until we slim down, or sports companies wake up and provide better-fitting running gear. And I bet I know which is the more likely.

So how should I tackle this during the programme?

I suggest you get your kit sorted in week one and stick to your winning formula, then perhaps go for a steady weight loss of a pound or two each week over the following four weeks if you can. You may also want to repeat this whole experiment after shifting a significant chunk of weight to see what changes in terms of your pace.

Try not to stress out too much about the scales though. Our focus is on speed, not weight loss and as I have said before you can get faster without seeing any change in your dress size. Trust me, I am living proof.

Even if you have no intention of losing weight make a note of your body weight at the start and your basic chest, waist and hip measurements too. A print-out from one of those full body-monitoring scales you find in Boots or in some gyms would be fantastic before and after the program as this would tell you about any changes in muscle mass, even if your overall weight hasn't changed.

I am not going to lie, during the pilot many women skipped this aspect of the programme. Maybe it was because they didn't have much lead-in time. Many felt like they were already eating well, were not in the right frame of mind to think about nutrition or weight loss simply wasn't part of the goal.

However, one of the ladies from my retreat has consistently been losing weight after finally having something click with her eating habits after a one to one session with our resident mindset and hypnotherapy coach, Donna Kenny.

She said:

"Improving my speed through training techniques has never felt achievable to me: if I can avoid pain then I generally do! So imagine my delight when my pace dropped from 8 ½ minute kilometres to 7 ½ minute kilometres after losing a stone in weight and not an interval session in sight!"

People often think because of my status as a plus-size runner I am either against weight loss in a rebellious, fat-positive way, or they think my whole campaign is about weight loss. Neither of these positions is true.

I believe aspirations for weight loss are a truly personal thing, and I support women's size goals whatever they may be.

For me the focus is always on health and happiness. For many women the relentless nature of extreme dieting plays havoc on their bodies and, more importantly, the impact on their mental health.

I am not a nutritionist nor an expert on safe and sustainable weightloss, I just know from my own experience and anecdotal evidence that there are some benefits for speed of carrying less weight as a runner; whether that be body fat or unnecessary layers of clothing.

Take some time to ponder on this chapter, and do what feels right for you.

Scream 3 – Spread 'Em

I believe it's better to be looked over than overlooked - **Mae West**

I found the above quote when I was just 16, I didn't even know who Mae West was, (She was an American film star and sex symbol known for her provocative double entendres, in case you didn't know either). But anyway I excitedly scribbled it down in my diary, not even sure I understood what it fully meant. I guessed it was supposed to be a little rebellious, because it struck a chord with my troubled teenage soul.

It is now a mantra I absolutely live my life by. If I think back to some of the situations I have found myself in as a plus-size runner, with all eyes on me, I would be an emotional wreck without the resilient attitude I have created for myself and backed with this ethos.

So now that we have got to know each other a bit better, can I ask you something a little bit personal?

Fab.

So, you know when you run?

Do you, erm, open your legs?

I mean when you run? Do you open your legs when you run?

Or do you just shuffle a bit, like something might actually drop out of your nether regions if you let even a small bit of air in between your thighs for a moment?

Huh? Me too!

I am a terrible shuffler. It's my default running style. At least it was before I started actively trying to improve my speed, that and a quest to get a photo with flying feet.

Flying Feet?

Yes, there is this thing in online running communities where you get bonus points for getting an action photo where there is clear air between the ground and you. It can turn into somewhat of an obsession.

I don't know about you, but I find it really interesting watching how other people run. It's a real hobby of mine and I think through my unhealthy interest in this and the subsequent research for this book I have discovered something so incredibly insightful that I may actually need to be awarded a Nobel prize or an MBE or something in the future.

Let me explain.

When I was initially scoping information for this chapter and looking for a suitable quote for the top bit about opening your legs, nothing came immediately to my mind. I really struggled to find something appropriate online, because come on let's face it, there are not many inspirational women going around the world effectively telling women to spread their legs.

What I found were memes such as the following:

"If your legs open up faster than Google's homepage, you're not girlfriend material"
"She's as good at spreading rumors as she is at spreading her legs"
"Do hugs, not drugs. Spread love, not legs"
"Your legs are like peanut butter; smooth, creamy and easy to spread"

I smiled at the first few and then I realised that the internet was filled to the brim with these misogynistic, so-called jokes, and it got me thinking that maybe there is a deeper-seated reason as to why so many female runners shuffle when they run.

We have all been conditioned over the years to basically keep our legs closed.
We are back to the days of riding side-saddle again, and we didn't even notice it.

Seriously, check it out next time you go to a mass participation event.

I, for sure, didn't really notice it until I started thinking about ways to improve my speed. So I started checking out other runners looking at the real minutiae of how they move to remind me of small adjustments I could possibly make to help me run better.

Have you ever looked at other runners in races and thought, "How the hell do you even run like that?" It's not that they might have terrible form it's just that we all run so very differently from one another. Just look at Paula Radcliffe and her almost horse-like trot, or Michael Johnson with his crazy upright sprint. And the uptight, yet full on running style of Forrest Gump - let's not even go there!

Do they know something I don't? Are they following perfect textbook form and technique? If I mimicked their style would I run faster? Well probably not because I am not them, my body doesn't move in the way their body does because my body moves in a way that is unique to me.

Cos it is my body after all.

So does that mean I have no chance of improving?

Of course not. But there are some basic adjustments you can make to your body as you run that should help you be more energy efficient, transferring it into power where you most need it.

There is a wealth of information already out there on improving your running technique, with experts who can go in to minute detail on gait and cadence, but I believe there is a simple checklist that you can go through whilst running to check that your form is not holding you back.

So let's do a head to toe inspection of your running body

Head – This might sound ridiculous, but I am going to say it anyway. SMILE. Seriously try it. During my first few years of running I grimaced like I had a bad case of wind, holding my face in such an unattractive manner it's no wonder people took the mickey out of me in public. But after seeing the worst race photo EVER, I asked myself "how do I even breathe like that?" and I tried smiling just slightly when I ran. I found that this released a whole heap of tension that I was holding in my face, allowing me to breathe more easily, while at the same time not look deranged.

Shoulders – Are you holding tension in your shoulders? A few circles every now and again will help you check, especially over a long distance or if you are particularly stressed. When assessing my form I also think about my posture at this point and try to picture a pair of Pat Butcher earrings hanging whilst I try to prevent them from resting on my shoulders. This helps me to stand tall instead of hunching over, which I am sometimes prone to as I tire. I also make sure I am not overcompensating and leaning too far back; a nice gentle lean into your run will help you move forward rather than upwards as you stride. Some people are so upright as they run I am surprised they don't move in reverse.

Core – When you think core, you often think of your tummy area, the thing that jiggles about as you run. You may think that there's not a lot to do except to hold it in and hope for the best. But actually having a strong core is more important than you would think. Your core is basically a set of muscles that wrap around your middle holding you upright. Your back muscles and obliques (the bits at the sides) are as equally important as your abdominals. Whilst running, check that you are in a comfortable controlled position of support, rather than holding the gut in so much that your shoulders rise and you have no room for oxygen, something I find leads to me getting a stitch. Work on your core frequently, the plank is THE best exercise for developing all aspects of your core, especially side planks if you can manage them.

Hips – If, like me, you carry a lot of weight around your hips then you may find that this is the first place you start to develop pain while running. You might even think that this area of your body doesn't really do much when you run, but you are wrong. The trouble could be in the outer hip area itself, or in your groin or buttocks where there is something called an IT band. This is what connects all these areas together, but can be a bit tricky to stretch. Knowing how to warm up all these areas well before you start will help improve flexibility, and focusing on widening your gait once you have started running could help propel you along at a faster pace too. I like to think of my legs like a pair of scissors when I run, the wider you open them the further you will travel with fewer movements.

Fingers – So what are you hands doing in all of this? Holding them stiffly by your sides is awkward and pumping them through the air a little hard core. You want to find somewhere in between those two extremes where your arm movements feel natural and your fingers can feel the air breeze through them. Whatever you do, have both hands empty to ensure good balance. You don't need a water bottle for 5 kilometres, neither should you be holding your phone in your hand. Keep an eye out for stress levels that build up in the arms and gently give your fingers a shake by the side of your legs every mile or so just to freshen things up. When you get to the last 500 metres or so now you can start pumping your arms, I prefer to keep a flat hand as opposed to a fist even if does make me look a little silly. It's amazing how much time you can make up in the final sprint.

Knees – So now we are getting to the business end of things. Keeping your legs moving effectively is crucial so the main thing is to keep them moving. DO NOT STOP. Addressing the form in your legs will lead to the most gains in terms of speed. But this doesn't necessarily mean you need to increase the rate at which your legs move. Thinking back to the analogy of the scissors from earlier, you want to keep up that length of stride in the groin area, but focus on long graceful strides where if possible both your feet come off the ground simultaneously. Making a conscious effort to lengthen your stride when tired stops you from doing that awful shuffle where the effort seems hardly worth it for the progress you seem to be making. I practise this on downhill sections, showing me how wide my stride could be if I only focused on this more.

Toes – Now this truly is where the magic takes place. I could have said feet, but actually it is specifically the toes that I am interested in. You will hear a lot about the positioning of your feet when you run, whether you have a heel or a toe strike, or even a mid foot strike. Regardless of where your foot lands when it hits the ground, by focusing on the power that you have in your toes you really can shift things up a gear. Every time you push your foot off the floor into the air, energy from your body is transferred into movement as you run. Sometimes though we waste that momentum by going up rather than forward; often we stop ourselves from fully embracing the power we have to push on, deploying instead a frustratingly safe shuffling motion that is easier to maintain.

So what do you actually want me to do for the purposes of the challenge?

This week, and throughout this experiment I want you to pay more attention to your technique and form than ever before and adjust accordingly. But mostly, if nothing else, I just want you to spread 'em more!

Try running some strides in your sessions; this is basically a term for running short blocks of exaggerated running steps where you correct your form. In the pilot we had the ladies doing these and they were met with mixed reviews.

"This was challenging for me, it felt awkward and made me self conscious"

"I tend to shuffle, so this really helped"

"I'm awful at this, but it makes such sense that it would work. So in the future I'm going to work on my ballerina leaps, no matter how silly I think I look"

We are all concerned with how we look to others, but remember you are in training to be a faster athlete and you may have to suffer for your sport.

Running stride and cadence is not something you can change overnight. It takes practice and perseverance and you might even notice unusual muscle soreness or joint discomfort as you transition from one running style to another, but it will be worth it in the long run.

The trick is to put some effort into tweaking it each time you run and to notice the small differences in pace when you employ these adjustments.

I find it useful when my Garmin beeps at me at each kilometre mark in a race to either do some strides or to think "head to toe, head to toe" and quickly run through that body assessment checklist.

Get out there and spread your legs ladies, just don't tell anyone I told you to.

Scream 4 – Vary your Speed

*The best things in life are often waiting for you at the exit ramp of your comfort zone - **Karen Salmansohn***

In the running world, interval training is probably the most talked about training technique for improving speed. But how many of us actually deploy it ourselves in our quest for speed? It's a shame because interval running can be quite good fun and can also break the monotony of your normal training routine.

I think for many newish runners the thought of moving between different speeds reminds us too much of the stop/starting we did when we first started running.

Getting to the point where you can run constantly over a 5K or 10K distance is a huge accomplishment. Many of us get caught up in the distance side of things and get used to focusing on not stopping, meandering along at the same pace, just happy to get around the course in one piece.

The problem with that is if you only have one speed setting (and no I am not mentioning the S word) and you never, ever run faster than your average running pace, after a while you will find you are stuck in a big fat plodding rut. Your body and your mind have simply got used to that pace. It could be down to a bit of laziness or even a bit of complacency, but whatever it's called in your books, it has to stop.

I have found it useful to think of my different running speeds as follows:

1. **Recovery Pace** – This is a steady pace I could run at forever if need be, the kind of pace where I could maintain a conversation with a friend.

2. **Regular Pace** – This is a consistent pace where I am required to work reasonably hard to keep it up, the type of pace I would normally run the majority a 5k or 10K race.
3. **Race Pace** – This is a pace where I am consciously pushing myself to run at a faster speed than normal, possibly the kind of pace you run at the start or finish of a race but one that is difficult to maintain for long periods of time.

Before focusing on improving my race times I worked on understanding these different pace settings and on being able to control them during a race. This increased awareness of my own speed settings gave me confidence to be able to push when my training called for it or take things down a notch if I really needed to.

What exactly is Interval Training?

At its core, interval training is just the act of speeding up and slowing down at different intervals within a set training session. What is so great about this technique though is its versatility as there are loads of different ways they can be done. Gaining or decreasing speed gradually, doing them based on set times or distances or even deploying a chance system, which is my favourite way of doing them. There are literally hundreds of variations so you will never get bored.

Why is it so effective?

When you up the pace and understand how running faster than normal makes your body feel, you gradually get more comfortable at running at that increased pace, but also you become less fearful of pushing beyond your current capabilities. There is of course also the more scientific response to this question, which is about increasing your threshold, stored muscle memory and generally gaining in fitness and strength with each session. Either way, if you include interval training in your running schedule enough you really will build momentum in terms of making those all important speed gains.

It is also useful to build confidence in terms of speeding up when you need to, like when trying to overtake people in a race or simply pedestrians as explained by one lady in my community:

"One of the really annoying things about only having one speed setting is not knowing how to get around that leisurely strolling couple and having to really speed up for 30-40 seconds so they don't have to stare at your bouncy butt for too long, and then thinking you might actually die as a result."

And what about this Jeff Galloway bloke who encourages walking breaks?

Lifetime runner, Galloway was a member of the 1972 US Olympic Team in the 10,000 metres event. He continues to run well into his 70s using the self-named technique which uses timed intervals of running and walking for long distance racing.

The method was designed in the 1970s, to help beginners start running with strategic walking breaks, allowing runners to control their own fatigue. There is a lot of research and anecdotal evidence that suggests that run/walk strategies are better for injury prevention and can actually help slower runners get faster race times over distances such as marathons and half marathons.

Is it interval training? Yes, in a way. And you can use the techniques in this book to improve your run segments, or to lower the amount of time you need to walk.

I am not a big fan of this technique as I prefer to listen to the signals of my body and to walk when I need to, rather than at set intervals. I use something called the 60 second rule instead.

What is the 60 second rule?

I first came across this when I headed off to Portugal to run a half marathon with my friend Mary who lived in Lisbon. This would be her first half marathon and as we sat the night before, carb loading with a spag bol and half a bottle of red wine, we discussed race strategies.

My daughter was only 8 months old at this point so my fitness wasn't brilliant and neither was my confidence in being able to run so far in the heat. Mary said she would walk, but only ever for 60 seconds at a time and by setting this rule she wouldn't ever let herself slack.

I tried it the following day.

I had no choice really as it was a flipping hot day and I was struggling from about the 7K point. I had no choice but to walk, but at the same time I wanted to get the race finished ASAP.

I loved this new technique. I never for a moment felt guilty for stopping and a minute seemed just about the right amount of time to gather my composure, catch my breath and start again.

It also inspired the "Walking is part of my race plan" slogan on one of our race vests that I sell to women around the world, which proved very popular.

So what's the challenge this week?

I want you to try out interval training or speed work if you prefer that term. So basically all you need to do is run slow, then run fast, then run slow, then run fast.

To break it down further for you, here are a few suggestions of different types of interval sessions you could try:

Remember to warm up beforehand and warm down afterwards to avoid injury.

- **Timed intervals** – This is the most basic of speed interval sessions. You decide on the length of your interval and you simply repeat over and over for a 20-minute period. 4 x 1 seems to work well to start with - running for four minutes at a steady pace and then running at your threshold pace for 60 seconds. This gives you plenty of time to recover, you want to run as fast as you possibly can in the fast bit, but be careful not to run too slowly during the slower section as this kind of defeats the object. As your fitness and stamina increase you could move to a 3 x 2 or even 5 x 5 ratio, building up your capacity to maintain your improved speed over a greater distance. You will need a basic watch with a stopwatch function for this to prompt the shift in tempo up and down. Some advanced watches have a specific setting which will beep at set intervals to let you know when to make that change.

- **Fartlek** – Don't worry this has nothing to do with gas, it's just a weird name for speed intervals that have a much more relaxed approach. So no set times or distances, more of a "let's have fun exploring and responding to my environment while running" kind of session. So you might use the lampposts along a street, or speed up and slow down between different trees in a park.

- **Chance** – Now this is my favourite type of speed session, and quite similar to Fartlek, but more about triggers and rules. You need to think about the route you are running and possible things you may see along the way that could act as prompts to change speed. You can choose static things like benches or local landmarks, but the more interesting approach is to choose moving objects such as people or dogs or even certain colored cars. You set your rules before you leave your house and then the rest is up to chance, or fate if you like. So it might be like for every person I pass that will be the trigger for my next speed interval, a red car might signal a 20 second blast, a dog on the path a reason to slow down. I use this trigger technique when I pass other runners to ensure I am running at my strongest.

- **Phone App** – There are lots of interval apps you can get on your mobile phones and many sports watches have programmable interval sessions on them. Personally I find these a bit of a distraction. It may be worth downloading a few of the free apps to see how you get on though. Something I have found useful however is an interval music track I downloaded from iTunes a few years ago. It is actually by Serena Williams the tennis star and although the music tracks are a bit dated now I always seem to improve my times when I play this. The track is 30 minutes long and includes a 5 minute warm up and a few minutes cool down; the main 20 minute session is just a series of music tracks with Serena encouraging you to "step it up" every few minutes.

So how often should I do these?

I would suggest focusing on intervals for at least one week to ensure you actually do them, but there's no reason not to try out as many variations of these as you like during the 60-day period, but at least one per week.

Remember you can combine these with a parkrun or a track session, but make sure your focus is on running consciously at different speeds during that session and not just plodding along.

I have often improved my parkrun time simply by deploying an interval approach, so it's definitely worth giving this a go over a race distance. The endorphins (feel good chemicals) set off by a speedy session combined with the added adrenaline of competing against others can be quite addictive, so be prepared to see results with this one.

This was the second most effective technique in the pilot. I didn't want to scare you off by putting it first in the book though.

"This helped a lot! I did lots of sprint interval sessions over the 8 weeks and I think this is what really helped me reach my 5% goal", said one lady.

"Yes, this works, but it's bloody hard work" said another.

She is right, but the effort you put in is completely proportionate to the improvement in your pace, so it's worth sticking with it.

Experiment.

Play.

See how it feels to push your body outside of its comfort zone.

Scream 5 – Be the master of your world

"A woman is like a tea bag – you never know how strong she is until she gets in hot water." **Eleanor Roosevelt**

Do you have an all-time favourite running route?

Are you a pavement pounder, or do you tend to run on trail?

Is your route somewhat of a safety blanket protecting you from the on look of strangers, or the thought of getting lost?

I guess what I am getting at is; do you run the same old circuit time and time again even though it no longer challenges or stimulates you?

It may even be holding you back because you are worried about being seen by people you know.

Or, like me, do you have a range of routes to suit your mood and the specifics of your current training needs?

As I already mentioned earlier, one of the most common reasons for never seeing any improvement in your running speed is failing to change up your training sessions and instead maintaining a habitual routine of humdrum "let's just get out there and get it over and done with" running.

But did you know that where you run is just as important as how you run and could be the difference between a good run and a bad run? It could actually be your running environment that is holding you back.

Could it be possible that where you run is slowing you down?

Maybe the physical infrastructure of your route, or maybe even the psychological associations you make to a place are obstacles in the way of your success.

This chapter is going to help you to really assess whether your routes are right for you and if a change could help you speed up a bit.

So here are some suggestions for checking this theory out; remember we are specifically interested in speed here, so although you might like meandering along by the river, if you have to stop every five minutes to make way for cyclists then this is not the route to get your next PB.

Here are some options for changing things up a bit:

Add Hills– Hills are great for building strength in your legs, but are hard work. Be mindful about when you schedule hill sessions into your weekly training routine. The day before your time trial maybe isn't that smart. Downhill running is good for stretching out your spread 'em stride too on the downhill.

Take out Hills - On days you want to go for speed, take out as many obvious obstacles as possible. I am not suggesting you cut out challenging routes all of the time, but be kind to yourself and give yourself a pancake flat course from time to time to simply push for speed. If you live somewhere hilly, jump in the car and drive somewhere flat for a change.

Routes with Pedestrians – Do you run better with an audience? If so carry on running in a busy spot like a park, but try to avoid city centres or busy thoroughfares where extra bodies are just going to get in your way. Running routes with other runners can be helpful especially if you can tag onto a faster runner's pace. If you feel uncomfortable running in public places you may need to address this. I find that if I run in a completely secluded place I have little to inspire me to run strong.

Other Runners – Use other people running with you as motivators. Try and stick with them. Or overtake even. In race settings if I am past the half way mark I play the 100 Game. It's simple, you count the people you overtake and subtract the people who overtake you. The aim of the game is to get to 100 before the finish line. It's a great motivator.

Running Surface – Think about the surface you are running on. Are you a pavement pounder, or do you have nice soft trails to run on? You might even want to try beach running which is fabulous for building strength. The point is what you run on will make a difference to your speed. So why not try out a few different types. Head to Scream Technique 7 for the best running surface of all for speed.

Travel to Run – Are you stuck in a rut with your speed where you run? Perhaps running in a new environment might speed you up. It's amazing what a change of scenery can do to your morale. I've run around Lake Geneva, around the island of Jamaica, and the streets of Berlin; each inspired me in different ways. Sometimes this is just a matter of taking your kit with you on your holidays, or you could plan a race somewhere exciting.

Explore what is around you – I bet you don't even have to travel that far to get that sense of doing a sightseeing run a lot closer to home. I bet you there are heaps of inspiring running routes less than an hours drive or train ride away. Why not be a bit adventurous and get out and explore what is on your doorstep?

Try a new parkrun – Ok so all parkrun courses are 5K, but actually aside from that, they are all very, very different. I am in the middle of 3 in East London. I call them: the fast one, the muddy one, and the hilly one. They each have a completely different vibe and I have recorded decent times at all 3. Be a parkrun tourist, it's great fun.

So what's the challenge this week?

It's quite simply to give some thought about your running routes and to schedule some alternatives to your normal running routes.

If you're super hardcore and want to challenge yourself, I would also schedule in a tough hill session too.

A hill session is not just a run up a few hills, it is a strategically planned and prepared session. It will have a knock on effect to your time trial that week and your need for rest and recovery afterwards. But the benefits will be great.

A typical hill session might look like this

- Locate a hill with reasonable gradient that takes at least 3 minutes to climb
- Warm up for 5 minutes or so on flat ground and do some dynamic stretches to get yourself mobile
- Power up the hill as fast as you can, leaning into the hill and using your arms to drive you
- Then jog down letting gravity assist as much as possible while catching your breath
- And repeat
- You want to spend 25-30 minutes doing this session
- Do a 5-minute cool down run

This session will be great for your cardio fitness and building strength in your legs. But be mindful that you are unlikely to break any speed records this week after a tough session like this.

It is so easy to avoid hill sessions because they are tough, or simply because you don't live near any, but maybe you need to look harder. I always used to say there were no hills near me, I have an underground car park where I live and that has the perfect slope for hill sprints.

In the pilot I got a real sense of the resistance to hill training:

"This really helped as I tend to avoid all hills in training, it helped me face my fears and actually do hills. Funnily enough it made running on the flat much easier afterwards too"

"This was tiring, but made me feel stronger"

On my annual retreat we did an epic hill session early one morning. The women didn't know they were doing hills, they were just told to leave their villa and walk up to the villa where the staff team were staying. They had to walk up an incline for fifteen minutes before they reached us, so they arrived a bit hot and sweaty before the session even started.

They easily guessed what the session was.
They only had to go to the top once, but once was plenty.

The session was run uphill to cone one, and walk back down, run to cone two and walk back down, and then run all the way to the top.

It was tough.

There was swearing.

There were protests.

There were tears.

But once everyone was up safely at the top of the hill, everyone felt incredible and we spent 20 minutes admiring the view and taking some super cool pictures.

Muhammad Ali once said,

"It isn't the mountains ahead to climb that wears you out; it's the pebble in your shoe."

I'm not sure what context this was said in, but I think for us in the running world the metaphorical pebble in our shoe is most definitely the uncomfortable feeling we have about pushing our self out of our comfort zone.

Most of what I do with the 'Too Fat to Run?' campaign is about empowering women to believe they can excel beyond their expectations. The fact is that the majority of my programme means they can do this in a safe way, without the requirement to run with others and to physically be challenged in the moment like with most running clubs.

Occasionally though I get to test this with real, actual people.

Ever year I run a half marathon training session in Hyde Park. In effect, it's a guided run with paced groups covering two 5 mile laps of the park. The first lap is always run at a super slow sociable pace, enjoying each other's company and the scenery. The second lap however is designed to challenge and I always bring in an assistant who can run faster than me.

One time I had a fab lady called Maya come and do the job. She was awesome. Supportive, but just a tad bossy and she helped the 6 women who chose the speedier group to run speeds they could only have dreamed of.

It was partly the excitement of running in Hyde Park and it was partly the impact of running in a pack and not wanting to let anyone down. It does show what can be achieved when you step outside of your comfort zone.

If we had advertised the fact the second pacing group would be running 8 minute miles, Maya probably would have been running them alone.

Running is one of those sports that as soon as you see progress, you see a new opportunity to improve; a new speed, distance or training goal. There is always room for improvement, always room to challenge your body further. It is what makes the sport so addictive.

'After climbing a great hill, one only finds that there are many more hills to climb.'
Nelson Mandela

Go find a whole heap of new hills ladies. Real or metaphorical, I don't care which. Who knows what you will find in yourself once you get to the top of each one?

Scream Technique 6 – Find a partner in crime

"Stop wearing your wishbone where your backbone ought to be."– **Elizabeth Gilbert**

One of the most frustrating things about being a pace-challenged (I.e. slower than average) runner is that a good percentage of the running population simply run too fast for you to keep up with. And even if you did come across someone who runs at your exact pace, as a newcomer to running even that comes with its own challenges.

I hated running with others when I first started out and avoided it like the plague for at least 5 years.

But why?

Mainly is because I didn't want to appear crap to other people. I care what other people think and nobody wants to have a witness to their obvious struggles, do they? There is so much psychology going on here, so many fears, so much anxiety:

- What will they think of me?
- Will they be frustrated with running so slow?
- Will they wish they never agreed to run with me?
- What if they leave me?
- What if they insist on me running faster?
- What if they get pissed off if I need to stop and walk?
- What if they are disgusted by the noises I make when I run?
- What if I smell?
- What if they hear me pass wind?

Seriously, these are all the things that go through your mind. Especially the one about farting, or is that just me?

They are basically all about our fear of judgment. We don't want to appear weak or look stupid. But these fears seriously hold us back when it comes to running, especially in terms of improving your speed.

There was such a shift for me when I swallowed my pride and finally joined a traditional running club in 2011, shortly after accepting a London Marathon place for 2012. I had been running for a long time by myself and although I had progressed in distance and to some extent speed, I knew the marathon distance was one I needed to respect, and I couldn't do it alone.

But the fear was incredible.

At the time I joined East London Runners they didn't have a beginner's session. Instead they encouraged people new to the sport to go along to a few local parkruns first, which makes perfect sense. But the problem is, even if you can consistently run 5k events, it doesn't mean you can keep up with even the slowest members of a running club.

It was relentlessly embarrassing turning up week after week on a Tuesday night and being the slowest member. It wasn't anything negative that anyone at the club did, it was just the fact that I was a lot, lot slower than everyone else. And nobody fatter or slower ever seemed to join.

I felt particularly bad having to run with the same volunteer each week, who was probably gagging to just get home and have his tea. In my case it was a lovely man called Don who is an absolute pillar of the club and a general all round nice guy. He never moaned, never made me feel like I had to run faster, he just plodded along beside me. He wasn't the most talkative of guys, which suited me fine too because running and talking has always been a struggle.

Occasionally, Frank, the Clubs chairman would take over from Don, which made for a pleasant change. But as a slightly faster runner and a talkative Scot, he was quite sneaky in his tactics to get me running a little faster, all done in the spirit of trying to be helpful as I moved through my marathon training plan.

He would get me chatting about my blog or my job on the Olympics (topics he knew I was enthusiastic about) and then he would discreetly increase the pace a little, and then a little bit more. I never really noticed until I got back to the club HQ and checked my Garmin.

"Wow! I ran how fast?"

My fear of running with others never disappeared completely though, but it did make me realise just how important sensible and clear communication is when considering running with others.

As I mentioned earlier, there is no value whatsoever in saying "I am a slow runner", that doesn't tell anyone anything. If anything, it is often used as a way of repelling potential running partners, or as a way of chickening out of opportunities to improve that arise.

The quest for the perfect running partner is like the search for the holy grail, or a partner who doesn't leave his socks on the floor; you are sure they are out there, the big question is will you ever find them? But if and when you do find them, boy oh boy does it feels like magic! So it's 100% worth the search. You can't just expect them to find you, you have to put yourself out there.

"It's so demoralising when you tell someone you are SLOW, but they don't believe you, and then they get frustrated with you while you are doing your best"

Listen, this is all about communication. If you communicate your ACTUAL SPEED and they don't take that on board, that's their issue not yours. There will always be unhelpful people out there who don't listen or comprehend.

I've just thought of a new mobile phone app for us 'pace-challenged' runners! It's like tinder, but to find the perfect running mate. I'll call it iPlod, or iSlog or something.

Imagine if people run around with electronic pacers flashing on their forehead, no, that would be silly. On their vest maybe, so you could identify their speed? It would be a bit like a mating call, a display of ability designed to attract the perfect partner.

The thing is even without these innovative ideas you have to be cunning, you have to keep an eye out for runners that look like they run a similar pace to you. start stalking your local parkrun results, and basically asking around about 5k PBs.

But it's not just speed that makes the perfect running mate. Your requirements will be different from mine, and the best way to ensure you find the perfect match is to be specific about what you want. Make a list. Just like Jane and Michael Banks did in their quest to find Mary Poppins. Who was practically perfect in every way.

Things you might want to consider;

- Location, how far away do they live from you?
- What is their average pace?
- Races, what are they training for?
- Frequency, how often do they run?
- How far do they want to run?
- What time of day or night do they train?
- Are they a talker? Will they get on your nerves?
- Are they supportive, will they be OK if you need to walk?
- Are they a good laugh, do you actually like them?
- Are they reliable...will they let you down?

Gosh, it's worse than trying to find a compatible life partner.

So yes it's not exactly easy and you may need to take a few for a test drive, as my dear nan used to say about real life dating - or courting as she would call it,

"Don't settle down too soon young lady, try out a whole heap of boys until you find the one you like".

But much like dating, it is a bit pot luck and a bit hard work so get used to talking about your pace and your desire for a running buddy. Take people up on their offer of running with you when it is offered.

Just remember to communicate and set some guidelines.

So what is the challenge this week?

I am not going to lie, this is likely to be the toughest week of them all and you are going to have to really push yourself to make this actually happen. In the pilot lots of women avoided this task altogether, but they did themselves a disservice because the ones that did absolutely saw more improvement.

Here are some options for your runs this week in order of effectiveness;

1. **Find a Virtual Buddy**
   This can work if you find someone with the same pace as you and really do commit to improving your time because they are keeping you accountable. This is the least effective though, because the act of physically running with someone does force you to run harder.

2. **Run in a group**
   This could be your running group or a training group you put together especially. Again, let them know your intention to run a little bit faster than normal, but don't go mad. This can

also work in a race setting, or at parkrun, simply by trying to keep up with the people around you. Or overtaking even.

3. **Ask a friend to pace you**
   This is the most effective option by far and involves asking someone to actually run with you with the specific purpose of helping you to run faster. This will take some good communication between you so that they understand your current pace and how much you wish to improve it by. Don't go mad, a few seconds faster per kilometre is plenty. Don't be afraid to ask someone to do this, plenty of runners will be more than happy to help. Think about where you might do this; a track is perfect for this kind of speed work.

Look I know this challenge is a hard one.

I know, honestly I do.

There are so many issues here, so many fears. But do you really want to be held back by your fears? And how many of these fears are based on reality? When asked what she felt about running with others, one of my ladies said,

"Urgghhh, it's the "encouragement" from fast people who double back to keep me company. I HATE that, just run your race, let me run mine. I don't need your pity, run your race, let me run mine"

How do we know it's pity though? Maybe they seriously want to make sure you are OK? Maybe they think it is the right thing to do, but in a completely unpatronising way? Or maybe they are happy as Larry running harder and further doing drop backs.

These are all stories we tell ourselves, they are our version of the truth, not the absolute truth. Remember we can change the narrative whenever we like.

Getting on top of this barrier is absolutely going to make running in a group easier, but you have to put in the work.

"Not being able to just arrange to go for training runs with friends is annoying because you just can't keep up and they just can't run as slowly as you".

Do you want to feel like this forever?

Maybe even without speeding up, just by communicating better you can find yourself some buddies at your speed and your quest for speed will be no longer.

Because actually all you wanted was some running friends and to feel like you weren't completely crap after all.

Right?

Scream Technique 7 – Run Track

Walking on to the springy red athletics track with my entire class aged 11 and a half is a memory I will never forget. The weird sensation underfoot, the scale of the place, the fact I'd seen similar venues on the TV.

Don't get me wrong, this wasn't a massive stadium with thousands of cheering fans. Nope, this was the track at the back of my local leisure centre, but that didn't dampen my spirits a single bit.

I'd always loved sports day and now I was in secondary school I couldn't wait to compete for my class against all the other forms in the year. And not in such stupid pursuits as the egg and spoon race, no, we were doing ATHLETICS!

"Now, you sure you can run Julie?" the PE teacher had said last week to me after a period 4 class.

"Yes Miss" I replied. Of course I could run.

I wasn't part of the school's athletics team, in fact I didn't do any after school sports activities, mainly because of my "challenging behaviour". Oh, and the fact I wasn't really any good at anything in particular.

You see, at my school you had to be good at sport to be picked for any of the school teams. Like Sarah Dodds, she was great at EVERYTHING. I mean she used to run back and forth to school for goodness sake, I'd watch her from the top deck of my bus each day. Nuts!

Anyways, back to sports day.

The atmosphere was fantastic as throughout the day small groups of students from across the year group got to compete against each other in a range of field and track sports, many of which I was seeing in real life for the very first time.

We were in the stands, me and my mates making up chants to support our friends and ignoring our teachers who insisted we stay in our seats at all times.

It was such a great day. So far removed from the strict Catholic school vibes we experienced back in the classroom. No, today we were free, or so it seemed.

The 800-meter run was the second from last race of the day. The 100-meter sprint finishing off the day, of course. I'd only been allowed to do this race because I'd promised the head of year I would buck up my ideas in class for the last few weeks of term, plus they were short on volunteers.

I didn't realise why this was until it was too late.

Walking from the stands down to the track in my brown PE skirt, yellow Aertex top and Ascot trainers, I felt like a superstar. All my mates were chanting my name, sure that I had this in the bag.

Our class was in second position over all, and we had the fastest girl in our year in our class, so all I had to do was finish in the top 5 and we would medal.

Easy!

I was a little baffled when I got onto the track and we weren't starting in a straight line, but I was positioned in lane 8 by some bloke, which meant I was ahead of everyone.

Great I thought.

I was told by one of the PE teachers to move over to the left hand side as soon as possible. I'd never done anything like this before so it was all a bit nerve-wracking.

But what the heck, I'd give it a go.

Sociology teacher Mr Shwaba (Or Shabba as we teased him, after a popular 90s Ragga artist) was the starter for the day and as he blew the horn thingy, I just started bombing it.

I wasn't really sure what I was doing though and kept looking behind me to see what everyone else was doing. And they were approaching me fast. I figured it was time to get into the lane closest to the grass, as that's where everyone else was now. But by the time I got there, everyone else was way ahead of me and reality started setting in.

It was only twice round the track, but everyone was super, super fast. It was starting to hurt my throat running this fast and I could already feel sweat dripping into my eyes.

I could see the girls in front of me turn round the bend, they made it look so easy, and all I could think was "shit I've got another lap of this track and I am already so far behind. My mates are gonna be well pissed off with me".

And that's when the idea came to me. I had to fake injury. So as I rounded the bend just before the stands, I purposely put my foot on the white edge of the track and pretended to trip.

Just enough to fall off balance.

For dramatic effect I put my head in my hands and started limping towards my Head of Year who was already shaking her head and looking at me in a disapproving manner.

My mates were cool about it and I got to sit with an ice pack and my leg elevated for the rest of the afternoon while medals were awarded.

That was the first and only time I ran a race on a running track and I wouldn't return for a further 20 years.

When is the last time you went to your local athletics track?

Well, it's not really the done thing really, is it if you are a slower than average runner?

Running tracks are for proper athletes. They are for the Mo Farahs and Usain Bolts of the world, right?

Wrong.

Running tracks are a public facility, often funded by the government or national lottery funding. They are considered a community resource and if we can't all have access to them there is something seriously wrong.

Besides, a lot of these places sit empty for most of the day, busy only at peak times, but deserted at others.

I remember the first time I went along to a "Track" session. I had been with my running club for well over a year. I knew they did a speed session at a track on a Monday night, but I was convinced it was only for the super speedy.

But then Grant, one of the coaches said something that turned that concept completely on it's head,

"Yes, of course there are fast people, but once they have overtaken you once nobody knows how far behind you are and at least you get to see other runners during the session"

He had a point, most of the sessions I did with my club I only saw the other runners in the Clubhouse before we got started or at the end of races if people hung around for post run drinks.

I am not going to lie; the first session was tough.

I'd lost all my marathon fitness after having my daughter and now I was training for another one, but starting from scratch. I couldn't even run one lap. But I simply walked when I needed to and did as much of the session as I could.

For the first few months I couldn't always follow the actual session as described, I just did my own thing, building up endurance and occasionally working on increasing my speed by running with other people.

Once I could do 3 or 4 laps without needing to walk though, that's when the devised sessions started to have an impact on my speed and endurance.

There are a million reasons to do track running, but health and safety considerations are not a bad place to start.

- For a start the surface is nice and flat and bouncy, so you are less likely to get injured or fall over.

- You don't need to stop for traffic. Faster runners will overtake you (just stay close to the inside lane unless told specifically to run in another lane)

- You are unlikely to ever get heckled at a running track. Most folk who hang around here are already involved in the sport somehow.

- Most tracks have flood lighting so you can run safely after dark

Am I tempting you with this info?

OK, so let's just suggest you might go along. You are probably thinking that you could possibly go along to your local track and run alone, but this can be quite boring. And you might be surprised to find that your local track has sessions that you can go along to. Even if they don't, you may happen across some friendly folk to try some sessions out with.

In all the years that I have been going track (and I must state I've never gone consistently) I have always seen improvements in both my confidence and my fitness, which in effect had a knock on effect to my running speed.

I would often find temporary running partners, people at a similar pace where they would push me to train a little harder, and occasionally someone would come along that was slightly slower than me and I would partner up with them to help motivate them instead. Yes, putting my superhero powers into action.

The other important factor for running track is that each session is likely to be different from the last.

Now I am no expert on devising track sessions, but I can share a few sessions with you, which can be replicated even away from a traditional track. Find yourself a park with a circular path, or even use a block in your neigbourhood, although all of the safety features of the track will be absent if you choose this way.

So what is the challenge for this week?

Well ideally I want you to locate your nearest track, enquire about their opening times, fees and whether they run beginners or open sessions.

Then of course I want you to go along and take part in a session.

If this is not a possibility for whatever reason, I want you to recreate a track session however you can, for the sole purpose of pushing your speed. Much like you did during interval week.

Here are 3 sessions you could try:

Threshold – A threshold or tempo run is a run where you are basically running faster than you normally would for a sustained distance. Where for example you are running at about 80% of your capacity. You still have to pace yourself, because you have to be able to last the duration. I would suggest starting out with around 400 metres, 3 or so minutes worth of running. You would then take a similar amount of time to catch your breath with either a recovery run or walk. Try not to stand still completely, you want to keep your muscles warm. Then do this again: 3 or 4 times or until you can't keep it up. I would say there are 2 main benefits of doing this session: physiological, i.e. you will get fitter and develop strength, but secondary you will gain confidence in pushing yourself harder. You may be surprised at how fast you can run and/or how long you can maintain it.

Pyramids – These take a little more brain power and are better done on a track due to the distance markings which make the maths a little easier. The concept is simple, you build up in distance to a climax and then come back down again. So for example, 400 metres, with a 200-meter recovery, then a 600 metres with a 200 recovery, then 800 metres with a recovery, then 600 metres with 200-meter recovery and then 400 meter with 200-meter recovery. Obviously as the distances increase you have to work harder to maintain the faster speeds. This is brilliant for improving overall fitness and the remembering of the distances keeps your brain active.

Yassos – Now we are getting a bit more technical, but this is a goodie. Created by running expert Bart Yasso, the session's full name is Yasso 800's, because that is the distance you will run. 800 metres, two times round the track. This is used to predict marathon times and although many of you are not aiming to run a marathon (YET) I still think this is a fun session to try. The basic premise is you run your 800-meter rep within a specific time frame: so for example when I was aiming for a 5 hour marathon, I would aim to do my 800 meter reps in 5 minutes. If marathon training, you would aim for 10 reps, with 400 metre recoveries in between. For us mere mortals I would simply say do as many as you can manage.

Look, I know these sessions sound a little bit scary. I did right at the start of this book promise that I wouldn't start getting all technical with runner's jargon. But there is something quite special about training in a specific way like this. Understanding why you are doing a particular session and being able to test your speed outside of a race setting.

What have you got to lose?

In the pilot of this programme, I left out track running all together as I was worried that nobody would give it a go. Plus, while I am being honest here, I felt like a bit of a fraud promoting this a technique as getting to my weekly Monday night track session had become near on impossible since becoming a single parent.

However, while putting this chapter together I figured I should head back, if for nothing more than research purposes, a token session to remind me why it is so useful.

What I didn't expect to do, 4 weeks after my 33.39 parkrun, was to take part in a Cooper Test which involved 12 minutes of sustained pace, which saw me running consistent sub 10 minute miles. I covered 1875 metres in that time and this was after a busy day running around after my daughter as well as an early morning CrossFit session so my legs were far from fresh.

Whenever I feel the need for speed, track never fails to disappoint. Just being in the company of other runners who want to see improvements inspires me to push harder than I normally would.

Also having coaches that instruct, support and advise is priceless. Well not exactly priceless; my session costs a whopping £1.50 because I am classed as a veteran (ha the cheek).

Tracks can of course be used for endurance, one of our runners in Greece used her local track to knock out a 16-mile training run. I would have gone mad by about mile 10 personally, but each to their own.

But for me track running is undoubtedly about speed. You can't help but push yourself and take your running more seriously while in this environment, even if it does feel a bit alien at first.

It's all about pulling those big girl pants up again, stepping into that athlete persona and giving it your best shot.

Just try it.

My 3 Special Secret Weapons

During the pilot phase I knocked an incredible 9 minutes and 12 seconds off my 5K time. This was disproportionately more than anyone else on this programme, with the average being around 3 minutes in the 8 week period.

Now there are a few possible reasons as to why this might be so:

Theory A

My baseline was phony.

When we started this programme at the end of August, I had just come out of a summer with very little activity, lots of summer festivals, too few training sessions and too many shandies. I did my baseline run on a regular training route I had done a million times, I ran as hard as I could given my current level of fitness. 43.27 is not the fastest I have ever run, but neither is it the slowest.

Theory B

I had more at stake than everyone else so more of an incentive to run faster.

Now there may be some truth in this one. Of course I wanted to improve my speed by a lot to prove these techniques worked. I had a book riding on it for a start. But the truth is, I didn't know if I could improve my speed by even 5%, let alone the almost 22% I managed in the end. I couldn't have predicted my improvement, because there were so many other factors at play.

These other deciding factors are what I really want to talk to you about in the final few chapters, in a hope that I might be able to inspire you further.

Giving you a few more tools for your running faster toolkit.

These concepts were not in my original book plan, but I could not simply leave them out. Because on reflection I think I did to some extent have a competitive advantage over the other ladies taking part in the pilot.

Even if I did not know it at the time. These 3 special secret weapons were,

- Strength Training
- The Law of Attraction
- Rest & Recovery

Secret Weapon 1 – Build Strength

*I didn't get there by wishing for it or hoping for it,
but by working for it* - **Estee Lauder**

I have always been a little scared of high intensity exercise. It's why running suits me because I can kind of just plod. It hasn't always been this way though, as a child I was a dancer, hitting the heights in my teenage years when I danced in a street dance crew called 8Pac. And trust me, we were anything but sedentary.

But as an adult, that fear of working my cardiovascular system to its limit got a bit unreasonable in case anyone laughed at my lack of fitness, which is stupidly counter productive right? I'd go to aerobics and always choose the easier option, at swimming it was breaststroke all the way and then maybe a length of front crawl at the end. it is probably the reason that I always avoided getting a personal trainer too as there really is nowhere to hide when it's one on one and you just know they are going to work you super hard.

And somehow I just wasn't really feeling that until one day, when the strength of my body was put to the test with horrifying results.

Just before I was due to run the London Marathon for the second time in 2015 whilst out celebrating my mum's 60th birthday, I managed to fall down the stairs of a double decker bus BACKWARDS. This was caused by a number of competing factors; a few cocktails in my system, an impatient bus driver on a busy night bus, my weak core, but mostly my weak upper body strength.

I was reaching the top of the stairs behind my sister as we headed to the top deck to find some seats when the bus suddenly and without warning pulled away sharply. I reached out for the pole to try and keep upright, but I didn't have enough strength to hold on and I went hurtling down the stairs hitting my head on the wall at the bottom.

I was severely concussed and had hurt my neck and back pretty badly, but I think the realisation of how much worse it could have been really hit home. And how I managed to run the marathon less than 10 days later I will never know.

But what I realised after that shocking incident is that despite the endurance and mental determination I had in bucket loads, what I really wanted for my body was to develop better strength and mobility and a confidence that I could cope better in situations when I can't afford to be weak.

And so I hatched a plan.

Earlier this year I started doing CrossFit. It's the most intense exercise class I have ever tried and stuck with and I've tried a few, trust me.

So what the hell is CrossFit?

"CrossFit is constantly varied, functional movements performed at high intensity, reflecting the best aspects of gymnastics, weightlifting, running, rowing and more.

These are the core movements of life. They move the largest loads the longest distances, so they are ideal for maximizing the amount of work done in the shortest time.

The more work you do in less time, or the higher the power output, the more intense the effort. By employing a constantly varied approach to training, functional movements and intensity lead to dramatic gains in fitness."

This is how the movement describes itself, but in Julie talk I would say CrossFit is simply a bloody good (but intense) workout which will challenge every aspect of your being (as it's physical, mental and emotional for sure). It will keep you on your toes too, because you never know what's coming.

Can we just talk about squats for a bit?

I like squats, heck we even have a 'Too Fat to Run?' Christmas squat challenge each year, but apparently I had been doing them all wrong. In part because my body just simply didn't have that range of mobility in it's hips. It sure as hell does now though.

If nothing else, doing 300 squats per week must have a positive impact on your running speed right?

Does it fit in with running training and the techniques in this book?

Well here is the point.

I had committed to doing CrossFit before I had decided to run this pilot. So I wasn't even sure if I would bother testing my own speed again. I mean I had done it the first time round and knocked off nearly twenty minutes.

I knew I wouldn't be able to fit 3 runs into my schedule on top of these CrossFit sessions, so the compromise was that I would run once a week. So that was one week testing that weeks technique and two 1 hour cross fit sessions.

It was all I could manage.

I was sore and tired all of the time. But I could tell I was building strength and endurance and I held on to the fact that it must help me in the long run.

There was something other than just the fitness aspect of this though.

Let me be frank.

I was consistently the fattest there.

I was the slowest and the weakest too.

There were people of all different builds and levels of fitness who take part, but I was the fattest and slowest without a doubt.

This took some adjustment.

It took a certain amount of grit and determination to keep showing up session after session knowing that I was pretty rubbish at everything, be that lifting my own body weight, touching my toes, or jumping on and off of a box.

In one rather embarrassing session an instructor asked if I was Ok and I burst into tears. I was just so tired physically and emotionally.

I went home early, but I was back the following day ready to jump back in.

Every time I turn up at CrossFit I know I am going to be pushed to my limits. Because the sessions are hard. And I don't do anything like this otherwise. My body is still adjusting to this level of workout and I haven't yet cracked my accompanying nutrition.

I don't think I have even lost any weight, but I would say my bum and thighs feel firmer and my back and shoulders look different too. Oh and I noticed muscles in my arms yesterday while holding on to the pole on the tube, so my body is definitely getting stronger.

How can you access the benefits of this without actually signing up to CrossFit?

Basically this is all about introducing a mixture of strength and high intensity training into your schedule.

How many sessions you decide on will depend on your level of fitness and how much time you have on your hands.

Swapping a run session for a cross training session, like for like makes most amount of sense to me, as this still gives you time to try the technique of the week and do the recommended time trial too.

This cross training session could be:

- Bootcamp Style Sessions
- Circuit Class
- BoxFit
- BodyPump
- Intensive Swimming (Front Crawl)
- Spin
- HIIT (High Intensity Interval Training)

By showing up and taking part in something as challenging as CrossFit or even a local bootcamp or circuit session as a larger, slower participant you change the dynamic of such sessions and perhaps even encourage other women like you to be brave enough to give it a go too.

CrossFit is bleeding hard work, but it teaches you how to push through mental barriers, build mental toughness and much much more.

Secret Weapon 2 – The Law of Attraction

Optimism is the faith that leads to achievement - **Helen Keller**

I am going to talk to you about something which you might think is a load of rubbish, but which over the last few years I have got more and more into and has 100% impacted on my running and more generally in my life.

It's called The Law of Attraction. Don't worry, it has nothing to do with bagging yourself a fella, or how attractive you look in your Lycra.

It is a concept that has been around since the early 19th century and came in to popular consciousness later in the 20th century with best-selling books such as 'Think and Grow Rich '(1937) by Napoleon Hill and 'You Can Heal Your Life' (1984) by Louise Hay. And then came the film: 'The Secret' which in 2007 garnered a whole heap of media attention.

So what is the Law of Attraction?

It is basically the name given to the concept that 'like attracts like', the idea that by focusing on positive or negative thoughts a person brings more positive or negative experiences into their life.

So say for example you walk around saying, "Oh I wish I wasn't so Fat", or "If I eat this I'm just going to get FAT", all the universe hears is the word "Fat", so it brings more of that in your direction, almost like you ordered it off a menu.

Sounds a bit bonkers right?

But after studying and testing some of these theories over the last year, I am starting to believe that there really is something in it.

OK, but what the hell has this got to do with my running?

Well at the beginning of this book I spoke about the use of the word SLOW, and how many recreational runners and newcomers to the sport consistently put their running efforts down.

If you are convinced you are slow and incapable of increasing your speed, chances are you will become a self fulfilling prophecy and perform at the level you expect yourself to.

Your effort will be restricted, the voices in your head will convince you that you need to walk, when you don't and you may even look forward to confirming your belief that it wasn't possible, "See, I told you I am just a slow runner"

But is it simply as easy as saying to yourself "I can run fast" and you will?

Well YES.

As crazy as it sounds this stuff works. In Scream Technique 1, I get you to tell your legs to move faster and to create a go faster mantra: this is the Law of Attraction in action.

During the pilot programme, I too tested these theories and in my race I called upon this law specifically in the final few kilometres to up my pace when my legs seriously did not want to keep moving,

Let me take you back to the start of that race and remind you how I used this.

It was a cold morning and I was glad that I brought gloves this time.

From the moment I got out of bed that morning I repeated my mantra to myself, "I am strong, I am fast" while lacing up my trainers, while brushing my teeth, while driving to Hackney Marshes.

I positioned myself further up the parkrun starting field than normal, hoping that I would at least run with slightly faster runners right from the off. I told myself I belonged here and that this was going to help me run faster.

This of course happened and a few minutes in to the run I glanced at my watch and saw a number 9 in the pace numbers. A NINE! I am a double figures kind of girl so I knew I was doing well.

But I was paying for it, my breathing was heavy and my legs were starting to hurt so I slowed down a bit as I approached the half way point. I looked at my watch and saw 16 minutes something so I knew I was on target and would meet my goal if only I could keep running.

But I was really hurting now and struggling to breathe.

I had to stop for a bit and felt quite ashamed for a moment as I walked across the uneven grass, but I refused to let the negative voices take over and I started batting them away, repeating positive messages instead.

As I headed back to the finish line, I knew the hard bit was still to come.

My pace was back in double figures again. 13 minute miles. 14 minute miles. I would lose all of that earlier speed advantage if I wasn't careful. So I thought back to the techniques I had been encouraging my ladies to use and started telling my legs to run faster.

I know. I know it sounds crazy, but it works! Seriously the voice in my head was saying:

Come on legs, get a move on, you have got this.

A lady who had passed me while I was walking was about 300 metres away and I thought she would make a good target to chase and the voices switched to:

You can get her, she will slow down, you can do it.

But she maintained her pace and I didn't make up any ground. I needed something else. Something to distract me from the fact this was really hard. Both physically and mentally. I kept glancing at my watch, but I wasn't able to do the maths to work out if I could beat my time. I couldn't risk it, I needed to keep pushing and I started repeating a new mantra in my head.

You are strong. This is easy. You've got this in the bag.

And seriously, this one was a winner. My stride lengthened, I felt instantly lighter and I found myself almost flying through the air rather than shuffling close to the ground which is often my go-to running style.

The 500 metres to go sign appeared like a beacon of hope at exactly the right time, and I knew it had taken me 3 minutes to reach this point on the way out. A glance at my watch informed me that I was on 31.05. It would be close, surely I couldn't run this last bit as fast? Or could I?

I took a deep breath, picked up my feet again and headed round the corner until I could finally see the finishing funnel. And then I gave it my all, pumping my arms and moving my legs as fast as I possibly could.

Great finish, I heard one of the volunteers say as I stopped my watch not daring to look at it.

I got my barcode scanned in autopilot mode and headed to my car for a much needed drink of water and a sit down and finally I drummed up the courage to looked at my watch.

33.40. WHAT?

I couldn't believe it. I had run my arse off, but I had absolutely put the effort in and seen the reward.

Had I made this improvement solely because of the training I had done in the lead up, or did my positive mental attitude on the day play a part in this somehow too? I know there have been plenty of occasions when I have headed to a race almost convinced I would be crap and we all know that negativity spreads faster than a cold sore between lovers. And yes you guessed it, low and behold I would have a rubbish race. Literally everything would go wrong.

It's not just about the race though, it's somehow about believing in your own capabilities and willing yourself to be the best version of yourself. Filling your mind with that positive soundtrack that I described earlier.

Beyoncé said:

"We have to reshape our own perception of how we view ourselves" and not only in our running world.

For many years I made fun of what I was doing with my blog. The running world thought I was a gimmick and in many ways I would play up to it and not take it too seriously.

Then I decided to up my game and start to believe in my abilities so I signed up to a Leadership in Running Fitness course, run by England Athletics.

I realised I knew just as much as everyone else there, maybe more about how to engage people who didn't enjoy running yet. Then at the end of the day as the instructors were closing the day, they asked us each to stand up and say what we hoped to get from our new qualification. They came to me first and I stood up and said:

"I want to be the world's leading running expert for plus-size runners."

People in the room laughed, but something inside me shifted and the following week I got some business cards printed, which said:

Julie Creffield, Plus-size Athlete, Campaigner, Author and Speaker

A few months later I was listed as one of 8 global plus-size fitness experts, the only one from Europe. So you see, what you believe is possible often comes into fruition. It requires some hard work too, but maybe the universe is listening to how we think and talk about ourselves. It's not like you have anything to lose by giving this a go.

And for the purposes of this challenge?

I know I have made reference to positive mindset throughout, but I just wanted to illustrate through this secret weapon that perhaps this is an area to explore even further.

I have known about it as a theory for many many years, but always felt like I wasn't the kind of person to believe in such concepts. So I never actively engaged in it. However, over the last 2 years I have got more and more involved, reading fabulous books like 'The Secret' by Rhonda Byrne and an incredible book by Pam Grout called 'E-Squared' which literally gives you DIY energy experiments that prove "your thoughts create your reality"

This way of thinking can be completely transformative. It can pull you out of negativity and depression and lead you into a space where you believe anything is possible, even if this is simply a case of reading positive affirmations from a piece of paper each day in front of a mirror.

Say something often enough and you will start to believe it.

Secret Weapon 3 – Rest and Recovery

When I'm tired, I rest. I say,
I can't be a superwoman today **Jade Pinkett Smith**

So we have talked a whole heap about running and putting in effort and of course speed during the course of this book, but let's instead talk a bit about not running, not being active, slowing things down to a complete standstill.

Let's talk about the concept of rest and recovery.

What's that I hear you say?

As women we really don't get enough downtime, do we? We don't get enough rest, we don't get enough sleep, generally we just don't prioritise our own self-care. There's always something else to be done on our scribbled or imagined to-do lists, somewhere our focus could be, a task which we have been putting off for far to long, it's never ending. Our work is never done.

Not to jump on the whole gender equality bandwagon again, but it does make you wonder if that is why men seem to be able to make improvements in their chosen sport more so than women. Remember 2 million fewer women than men play sport in the UK. Maybe that's because we are all too flipping busy looking after everyone else.

So let's for argument's sake say you are running three times a week, each time for less than an hour. You might not think that your body needs to rest and recover, but it does, especially if you are not getting enough sleep and rest generally.

Your muscles need time to rest and repair, and you basically need to re-energise for the next week's run. Because otherwise before you know it you will be run down, injured or simply running on empty.

If you look at the training plans of professional athletes, you will notice that rest days are scheduled in with the same importance as weight sessions or tempo runs. But I know how hectic my life can be. Sometimes a rest day means just not doing any structured exercise, yet I can still be found covering 20,000 steps, lifting my 4-year-old in and out of the car and doing the laundry and housework, so I am hardly having a rest.

When athletes in Kenya's famous marathon training camps rest, they REALLY rest. They literally do nothing but eat, lounge about and sleep. You won't find them popping to the supermarket or off socialising with their friends. They understand the importance of just doing nothing in order to let the body fully recuperate.

OK so you are not an elite endurance athlete. But you are an athlete so basically you need to channel your inner Kenyan and have a bloody rest day every now and again.

No matter how much exercise you are doing, you still need at least one day each week when you get a rest and don't do anything remotely arduous.

Now you might be thinking: yeah right Julie, it's alright for you to say that. How the hell am I supposed to get time to rest, have you seen my schedule? My to do list? My ironing pile?

In my last book, 'New Year Same You' I talk at length about how us women tend to take on far too much and in the process fail to prioritise our own health and happiness over and above the needs of everyone else.

Maybe it's fine time you addressed this disproportionate imbalance, meaning that during this 60 day programme you will be more explicit with your loved ones about what you actually need: more time to yourself for recovery.

Perhaps you will switch your superhero duties from mother, wife, partner, daughter, friend, colleague to simply being YOU, putting YOU first, pleasing YOU and only YOU in your desire to improve your speed.

Ideas for some down time:

- Marathon movie watching session
- Regular massages either professional or otherwise
- A lay in once a week
- A super early night to bed
- Some morning meditation or gentle yoga
- A weekly extended soak in the tub
- A half day on the sofa reading
- A spa day - ooohh wouldn't that be nice!

I actually schedule Fridays in my work diary as a ME DAY, ok so I work for myself and have the luxury to do this. But I also have a 4-year-old and am a single parent, so if I don't schedule time for recovery in, it just doesn't happen. Weekends are not a break for me, as I am still up super early and often I am racing.

It doesn't have to be a whole day, a 4-hour mini break in your week will do you the world of good.

Or even a 15-minute check in once a day.

I do something at 3pm everyday to make sure I am listening to what my body needs.

I call it my 3pm Pit Stop.

I have an alarm set on my phone for 3pm everyday of the week, and when it sounds I ask myself the following questions:

- Am I thirsty?
- Am I hungry?
- Am I tired?
- Am I sad?
- Do I have any pain anywhere?
- Do I need fresh air?
- Do I need to speak to someone?

What happens if I simply can't do this?

Chances are without rest and recovery your progress is likely to be slower. You will also be more prone to injury, illness and general fatigue.

Signs of fatigue include unshakable tiredness, low energy levels, unexplained aches and pains.

Also, when your body is overwhelmed by training you are likely to get cranky too as your body produces hormones like cortisol that can cause irritability or anxiety and prevent weight loss too. Funny that. Stress also halts chemicals like dopamine, the happy drug.

If you are already run down or unwell, or even just on your period, your need for energy to refuel your immune system will increase, as it will now be working overtime. This means fewer resources available for recovering from training.

Try some active recovery tactics

Maybe you just can't keep still.

Here are some examples of rest and recovery activities that will still help:

- Walking
- Static stretching exercises (make sure you are warm though)
- Dynamic stretching, think YOGA
- Gentle swimming
- Water running
- Riding a bike for leisure.

You only have one body. It is the vessel that houses you. It makes sense to look after it.

Finding the balance between training hard and resting well is something we all need to work towards. Perhaps use the 60 day challenge to really try practising this.

Extra Race Day Tactics

I know you have this running faster thing under control now, but just in case you need a bit more support or a few more ideas of how to shave off those all important seconds when you attempt your fastest 5K yet, here are my top 10 tips for "Smashing that PB" come race day.

1. **Wear the right kit.** I mentioned this before, but seriously this can make a huge difference. When racing I wear my best tights, a top that doesn't ride up, my fave sports bra adjusted properly, my shoes tied up properly, a head buff to keep hair out of face and sweat too, and gloves to keep my hands warm. I am often cold at the start line, but this will stop me from walking. It's only 5K after all and running fast will keep me warm.

2. **Run with a pacer.** Now this is not for everyone, but if you can find a faster runner than you and get them to run at the speed you want to finish the race in then they do all the speed adjustments and you just need to keep up.

3. **Position yourself right**. I tend to do my speed test runs at parkrun and rather than starting right at the back I am position myself a little further ahead. And OK people will overtake me, but the likelihood is I will try and keep up with them for as long as possible. Don't get stuck behind a group, don't be afraid to overtake.

4. **Ignore everyone else**. Do not concern yourself with what other people think of you, perhaps you are worried about others seeing you running faster than normal or putting in extra effort. This is your challenge!

5. **Use your sports watch**. So often we only look at our watch when we are switching it on and off, get used to glancing at it every 60 seconds or so, use it as a prompt to speed up. Also keep an eye on how much more distance you have left and when you have 1K to go, try and up the pace a little if you can.

6. **Overtake others.** Try not to get overtaken, try to overtake. Play it like a game and keep a count of how many people you have passed, but subtract for those that pass you. Cat and Mouse is a fab way of keeping the pace up

7. **Remember the 60 second rule**. If you are using walking breaks (which is fine) only ever walk for 60 seconds and then start again. You can use this to slow the pace down if you feel you want to walk, take the foot off the pedal for a minute if you feel like you can't maintain the pace, but speed up again after the 60 seconds.

8. **Tell your legs to go faster**. This works I swear, shout it out loud if need be.

9. **Sprint Finish.** In the last 200 metres you know you are almost done, you could shave 10 seconds or so just here, so pump those arms as hard as you can and open your stride as you come home in glorious style

10. **Take a photo of your post run face immediately.** I want to see the sweatiness and those beaming red faces. I want pictures of your results too, either your sports watch or the numbers scribbled on a piece of paper, upload them to Facebook, Instagram or Twitter. I'd love to see them.

I know you can do it. You just need to do the work!

Good luck. Now go smash that PB.

Conclusion

I have been running for close to 40 years, since I was about 11 months old according to my mum.

But I have been participating in the actual sport of running for 12 or so glorious years. Yet even me, someone who has run marathons, a fitness blogger who has numerous books on the subject, someone who coaches other women to run...

I still sometimes don't feel like a proper runner.

It's ridiculous.

And it is totally about speed.

Do you know how many times someone has made an off hand comment like:

"Oh you will get faster once you have been doing it for a while".

Or

"Perhaps you should think about signing up for a 5K as a goal to help you improve".

I bite my tongue, even though all I want to do is scream and shout that I am not a beginner and that my current speed has little bearing on my enjoyment of the sport, and neither should it disqualify me from participating in whichever way I see fit.

People just make assumptions that if you are slow and overweight, then you are a beginner and, of course, your only goal must be to get faster and slimmer. And perhaps for some women it is.

But for plenty of women it is not!

All I know is I have 40,000 followers on social media who have somehow been inspired by the Too Fat to Run concept and hundreds of women who take part in my programmes tell me weight loss and speed are not the key drivers for them participating in the sport.

It is so much more complex than that.

I love the sport of running. But I get so frustrated by the hierarchies that still exist. The competitive structures that are in place that prevent so many people from progressing further in the sport. Even parkrun, a movement that I absolutely adore, is still seen by many women as the scariest thing on earth to do on a Saturday morning run with an audience and a digital record of time.

Something needs to shift.

And call me pessimistic, but I don't think that shift is coming from the powers that be in the sport, the running clubs, the race organisers, or the big clothing brands they are unlikely to change much in the next few years.

No, this shift is a deep level shift in consciousness which is very much coming from the ground up. You only have to see the rise in online running communities such as Run Dem Crew and Run Mummy Run. We are finding our own way of doing things and not asking permission anymore.

Runners are often considered a tribe, but we are very much a fragmented tribe, or more often than not we are members of multiple tribes within the running world. And there is a place for all of us. It's not like the pink tutu-wearing Race for Lifers have any kind of negative effect on the harriers speeding their way towards their next big race. We can coexist side by side quite happily, and possibly even complement each other.

Nobody has the monopoly on running as a sport or as a pastime, it belongs to all of us. It is ours to cherish, to nurture, to keep safe for future generations. We each have a role to play in embodying the shared values that many runners have and to be the light for others coming into the community.

Yes, we hear negative stories of race cut-off-times and the annual debates about walkers at the big city marathons, but come on! The sport is diversifying and growing exponentially and it marks exciting times for us all.

We need to pull ourselves out of the negative ruts we sometimes find ourselves in. Stop being all "poor me, poor me" about our lack of pace or fitness and turn that desire to be better, to be stronger and more determined to make changes.

Running faster is not going to automatically make you feel like a "Proper Runner", I mean even with my significant improvements with speed using these techniques, I am still very much a back-of-the-pack runner and that is cool with me.

I think it runs deeper than this though.

Taking the time to focus on improvements gives you an inner sense of achievement and acknowledges your desire to be taken more seriously as a runner, even if just by yourself.

That self-awareness is where the magic happens ladies.

Achieving a speed goal is much like achieving a weight loss goal. The number is not what is important. Life is not better all of a sudden because you have reached that magic number.

'Oh I'll be happy when I am a size 12'. Will you heck.

You have to show gratitude and be at peace with where you are right now if you ever want to find true happiness within yourself. The journey teaches you things about yourself which are invaluable and far more enriching than the final destination. Because chances are, once you get your sub 30 5K there will be some other goal, some other desire you will want to start working towards.

Give thanks that you are able to run at whatever pace. Thank your body for giving you that ability. Thank your legs for carrying you and your heart and lungs for powering you, your heart and soul for helping you believe it is even possible.

Gratitude is so important, but also having appropriate role models to draw inspiration from is vital too.

There seriously is no point looking at the fastest runners in your running club for inspiration, I've tried. As lovely as these people are, they do not live in my body, they do not live my life. If anything they just confirm that nagging voice in my head that says "Julie you will never be good enough".

Did you know in a previous life I worked as a project manager on the London 2012 Olympic Games? Yep I did. For 8 or so years I worked in various roles helping to inspire local people to get involved with the games, to embrace the Olympic and Paralympic values of

- Friendship
- Respect
- Excellence
- Determination
- Inspiration
- Courage
- Equality

I spent close to a decade with these values knocking around in my head, designing programmes for old age pensioners and school children alike. It also involved working with politicians to get them all singing from the same sheet and basically inspiring people to be the best versions of themselves, even if for only a few weeks over one summer.

It's amazing what a bit of encouragement and inspiration can do.

You should have seen what my piece of East London was like during that incredible summer. Local people voluntarily acting as hosts and tour guides, welcoming people from all over the world, actually smiling and speaking to each other.

An army of 70,000 volunteers giving up their summer to be part of something special, much like the thousands of volunteers who get up each Saturday morning to support parkruns across the country. They do it because they want to be a part of something bigger than themselves.

I was extremely privileged during this part of my career to meet many Olympic and Paralympic stars. A week into one job I did for a government organisation I managed to get stuck in a lift with Sir Steve Redgrave which was highly embarrassing. One day, while volunteering in the anti-doping team in the athletes' village, the whole Jamaican sprint team walked in with Usain Bolt looking incredibly nervous and shy.

Over the years I have met:

Paula Radcliffe
Mo Farrah
Tessa Sanderson
Justin Gatlin
Chris Akabusi
Victoria Pendleton

Tanni Grey-Thompson
Ryan Lockte
Kelly Holmes
Jo Pavey
Christine Ohuruogu
Sharron Davies
Dave Moorcroft
Sebastian Coe
Jonathan Edwards
Brendan Foster
Sally Gunnell
And many, many more.

Now I don't reel off these names to show off and neither do I credit meeting any of these phenomenal sports people with having any real impact on my own running.

Harsh but true.

Of course I respect individually what they have each achieved.

I look at the dedication and commitment they show to their sport. But in many ways these individuals are a million miles away from the kind of athlete I am, or the kind of athletes I deal with.

These athletes dedicate their lives to their chosen sport. They obviously had some natural ability to start with, but they go on to train full time, they have a team of experts supporting their journey and therefore it is impossible to make any kind of comparison to every day normal people.

Rania Rempouli, a Greek Olympic marathon runner, said of non-professional marathon runners 'In my eyes you are the heroes. You are the ones having everyday jobs and lives and getting up at 5 o'clock in the morning to get your training run in before work. I have the luxury of just running and training.'

Professional athletes are in many ways our super human, super heroes. Do they inspire us? Hmmm yeah, but not half as much I believe as the people we see around us in our every day lives that are doing extraordinary things.

I see it day in day out, I get emails from women all over the world saying "I did this, because I saw you do it", "I started to believe in myself because you have shown me that normal people can do these kind of things too"

The #ThisGirlCan campaign was a fabulous example of peer to peer inspiration. Also a great pilot programme in Derby called "I will if you will" did exactly what the title suggested, using word of mouth and imagery of every day local women to show what is possible.

So every time you go out in public and run you are the embodiment of this movement. You may not feel like a superhero most days, but with each footstep you are potentially changing someone else's life. Doesn't that feel empowering?

You are a superhero, you just need to start believing it.

I know I have talked a lot about superheros and villains in this book, perhaps depicting the running landscape as a bit of an aggressive battleground. Well I suppose it's better than painting a picture that is all rosy and some kind of fairy tale story, where us ladies are all seen as princesses.

I feel so strongly about the damage caused by young girls' obsession with being a Princess and it is something I am constantly working on when it comes to the way I talk to my 4-year-old daughter.

Of course she is obsessed with Disney. It's pretty hard to escape it, we had at least 12 months of Frozen replays for goodness sake and she loves nothing more than to dress up as a princess with her friends. I, of course, don't want to take this joy away from her, but equally I am also teaching her to be a warrior, to be empowered, to make choices, to be strong and capable and resilient.

Recently however, I discovered a perfect fairy tale film which I really don't mind watching with Rose over and over again. It's the latest film version of Cinderella, starring Lily James as Ella, a really beautiful yet clever film with such an unusual insight into the real concept of happy ever after.

Early on in the film when her mother is on her death bed the young Ella is told, "Be kind and have courage". Hey, that's not a bad motto to live your life by. Right? We could all do with a little more kindness and some encouragement to face our fears in life.

Let's face it, Cinderella has a pretty shitty life doesn't she? Yet she finds a way to keep positive through it all, singing and dreaming away the days and being kind to everyone she comes across. You never see her speak badly to those who treat her badly, retaliating only ever gives away your power anyway. I learned that the hard way trying to respond to hecklers. You never come out on top. EVER!

I think the biggest message in this film though is simply believing in a bit of magic from time to time. We don't need to know how things are going to change, or even why. We just need to have faith that they will, and accept that sometimes unexpected things take place and it is our job to welcome them into our world with gratitude.

Perhaps we have to be our own fairy godmother and wave our own magic wand to transform what is already around us.

The bottom line is, if we are not the villains of the running world, and we are not the superheroes, who are we in this story, the victims?

Hell to the NO!!!

Yes, life can be hard sometimes for all of us, but taking on a poor me attitude serves nobody. We live in challenging times on so many levels and for many of us running can seem like just another chore to add to our list, or worse still just not important enough in the grand scheme of things.

But we have a choice to continue seeing it like that, or to see it as the gift that it is....an opportunity to go on a great adventure. A quest of self discovery, alone or with pals. Exciting right?

Thousands of women wish they could run, wish they could reap the many rewards it brings or could find the strength to get started, and we already have. And it is not all bad is it? Just think of the awesome memories and experiences we have created for ourselves, the friends we have made and the difference we have made to our all-round health.

Look, there is no denying it, we have a huge problem with inactivity globally.

Obesity is not the problem, mass inactivity is. Fatness is just the side effect of it and even if the overweight and inactive populations of the world failed to lose a single pound, but started exercising 3 times a week at a reasonable intensity, then they improve their chances of having to deal with (or maybe just limit the effect) more than 20 lifestyle-related diseases regardless of their current weight.

We need to normalise sport for adult women. It can't be something the skinny, attractive women do in matching kit. For most of us running is not pretty. We sweat, we grunt, we chafe, we moan, we get shin splints, shit some of us even wet ourselves occasionally.

That is the reality of running for most of us, not the perfect images we see in glossy marketing campaigns trying to get us all exercising. Why don't we just start accepting the truth of it all?

It's how I couldn't care less about letting my fat hang out when I run and not wearing perfectly matched kit...cos let's face it, it's bloody hard finding nice stuff that actually fits. It's why I talk about my embarrassing experiences and post sweaty, unflattering pictures.

This is how it fucking looks peeps.

You bought this book because you wanted to improve your speed and it will help you do exactly that.

But you have to do the work.

Do the work and also set yourself realistic goals and be OK with whatever you manage to achieve.

The reality is that my plus-size, 38-year-old body will probably never run a sub 45 minute 10K now and that is OK with me. No, really, it is.

I don't run for the times on my watch. I run for the experience, the lifestyle and as cheesy as it sounds, I run to have the time of my life. Which so often I do. And anyway, I've only ever come last that one time.

I wish you every success with your pursuit to improve your speed and I hope you smash your goals during the 60-day challenge, but actually I know the techniques and concepts in this book will stay with you beyond that.

I believe in you.

I know you can do it.

So start telling yourself that NOW

The stories we tell ourselves are what define us, so if it is a shitty story change the script.

Decide this is the way forward, and start stepping one foot in front of the other towards the direction of that success.

Ask your body, tell your body and encourage your body to run faster.

If you tell it enough it will listen and if it doesn't that's when you need to up your game and make it listen.

Be kind to yourself, be happy with your progress and have courage to push further to find the stronger version of yourself.

Run Strong
Run Fast
Run Happy

And don't forget to share your progress with me, I am a nosey cow like that.

Love always,

Julie

Acknowledgements

Saying an official thank you is something we often do in life as a matter of course and too often the words simply don't do justice to the people you truly want to express gratitude for.

In most books authors thank their commissioning editors, their agents and their significant other half. I have none of these in place right now, so my thanks instead are reserved for the hundreds and thousands of women across the globe that support my work.

The women that inspire me daily, pick me up when I am down and continue to offer their help in practical ways such as proof reading my books, or taking over social media for me during busy points. Women are an incredible force to be reckoned with when they are on a mission to improve the world.

You often hear people talk about Tribes; I like to think of my supporters more as an awe-inspiring herd, a group on a similar path, sticking with each other and supporting one another on this sometimes challenging path.

This book simply wouldn't have been completed without the help of my women.

Firstly, my Clubhouse ladies who encouraged me to get the old manuscript back out and give it a second shot at bringing it into fruition. The practical help in editing the book from Cass and Joey helping on social media to promote it. I could actually list so many of the characters from my online club for the acts of kindness they have shown to me, but I'd be here all day.

Then there were the 100 women who signed up (and paid) to take part in my 8 week pilot to test the programme. I made plenty of mistakes in this online programme, many that I simply had to hold my hands up and apologise for, but the women never left my side, feeding back on what worked and what didn't and offering their wisdom on how to make the programme better.

In life I never strive for perfection, for a start life is too short for that. When you have an important message to share people don't tend to mind too much what format it comes in or if it is a little rough around the edges.

The other person I must show appreciation for is my sister Jennie, my biggest supporter. She always believes in me, never questions my desire to want more in life and she is always the first to offer practical support to help me get there often in the form of childcare. Just as well Rose likes her, else we would be in trouble.

Thank you doesn't do justice to any of this.
Thank you isn't enough, it's never enough.
But it's all I have. So from the bottom of my heart, I thank you all.

For your belief
For your support
For your custom

I guess the final thanks has to go to my very own body. The body which I spent so many years actively hating, a body which has been patient with me, has taught me things about me, the real me, not just its casing.

Gratitude works wonders on self-esteem and feelings of self-worth. Try it. Next time you see an improvement in your running, say thank you to your legs for getting you round and your heart for doing its marvelous job. And even on those days the run doesn't go to plan, still say thank you.

If you find this eBook useful then please tweet about it using #TFTRSpeed or #TFTRScream, blog about it or mention it to your friends and family.

Get in touch to let me know what you thought about the suggestions and how you are getting along with your running. I'd love to know how these 7 techniques have helped you reach your speed related goals.

Remember there are millions of people just like you and me who would love to be able to run faster, but just don't know how. So help them out and tell them about this book.

I am @fattymustrun on Twitter and you can follow my blog www.thefatgirlsguidetorunning.com or get involved with a fantastic community of plus-sized runners at www.facebook.com/thefatgirlsguidetorunning

As a special thank you for being a reader, use discount code SPEED for 20% off our online programme where you will find accountability and support from women just like you. www.toofattorun.co.uk/shop/scream-if-you-want-to-go-faster/

Thank you for being part of the 'Too Fat to Run?' revolution.

The Clubhouse

If you are looking to join an online friendly running club with members from all over the world and of all abilities The Clubhouse is for you. Whether you have just started or you are training for a marathon, the training support and camaraderie is second to none, and there's nothing like a virtual kick up the arse to keep you accountable.

The Clubhouse costs just £59 for the year and you sign up via the website **www.toofattorun.co.uk/join-the-Clubhouse**

Other Books by Julie Creffield

New Year, Same You
5 Weeks to 5K
How to Run with a Baby
Slouch to 10K
Getting Past the First 30 Seconds

Printed in Great Britain
by Amazon